About the author

Pamela Cunnington was an architect in private practice and for seventeen
years the Historic Buildings Officer for the county of Dorset. She was a
Lethaby Scholar of the Society for the Protection of Ancient Buildings.
Her books on domestic architecture are well known, and include
Care for Our Houses and *Change of Use*. Her lifelong interest in
church buildings resulted in *How Old is That Church?*, the
companion volume to *How Old is Your House?*

How Old is Your House?

Pamela Cunnington

Marston House

© 1980, 1982, 1999, Estate of Pamela Cunnington

First published in 1980
First paperback edition, 1988
2nd paperback edition, revised 1999
Reprinted 2002
published by Marston House,
Marston Magna, Yeovil, BA22 8DH

British Cataloguing-in-Publication Data

A catalogue record for this book is available from the British Library.

ISBN 1 899296 08 5

Most photographs and all line drawings by the author

Printed in China by Regent Publishing Services

Contents

Foreword

The history of a house can be considered as the history of the people who have lived in it. Conversely, the people who have lived there have shaped its history and often its appearance.

England has a multitude of stately homes and grand houses which are not short of historians. Often they like to link the events in the lives of their notable occupants with the changes and developments in the architecture. The evolution and the appearance of more humble buildings has much less documentary evidence, but no less history. The unravelling of the past of what are now universally known as vernacular houses has, since Pamela Cunnington wrote this book in 1980, a host of passionate followers. There are popular television and radio series, specialist magazines and books as well as building preservation trusts and co-ordinating bodies; and there are museums like the Weald and Downland Museum, Sussex, and the Geffrye Museum in Shoreditch, all concerned with the well-being of old buildings of all types.

That non-specialists are now better informed about the buildings which they cherish must be an improvement on generations of neglect and lack of respect. But too much loving can be a bad thing, and in the course of restoring and renovating an old house its integrity can by degrees be taken to pieces. Early generations sought only to modernise. Seventeenth and eighteenth century 'modernisation' gave a fourth dimension to our town and country architecture as part of a moving spectrum of which we, at the turn of the millenium, are just the current leading edge.

The first stage in respecting ancient buildings must be to understand the structure, not just in mechanical terms, but also in a social context – history, geology, economics, geography, fashion and other aspects of the lives of ordinary people all find their expression in the homes in which the people lived, and once research begins on the past of a building, expectations and enthusiasm gather pace.

In helping individuals to understand their properties, Pamela

Foreword

Cunnington, architect and Historic Buildings Officer, was an inspiring guide. By providing such an accessible yet scholarly handbook in *How Old is Your House?* her own enthusiasm has already communicated to a generation of readers who respond to old buildings. As an architectural historian, Pamela was much respected; as an Historic Buildings Officer, she was indomitable in her defence and protection of the humble house which lay in the way of a developer or of development plans. We, her disciples, have much to be thankful for, especially in this, the first of the four books she wrote in celebration and protection of old houses which may seem ordinary, but are extraordinary.

Tony Birks

Introduction

My introduction to architecture was an interest in old churches inspired by my grandfather who, though not an architect, would probably have described himself as an ecclesiologist. This led on to an interest in old buildings including, of course, houses. Much of my work as an architect has been concerned with the care of historic buildings, first in private practice and more recently in local government. During the last ten years I have been working in south-west England, which contains many interesting smaller and medium sized houses. Furthermore, the very nature of my work for the Dorset County Council has enabled me to visit and study the domestic architecture of the county to an extent which otherwise would probably not have been possible.

One fact which all this has brought home to me is that the smaller houses in the towns and countryside are often older and more interesting than they first appear. Until comparatively recently they have not received anything like the detailed study given to larger houses, or to churches. But the position is now changing. It is being realised that just as the smaller parish churches are, in their way, as important as the cathedrals and abbeys, so the smaller houses are as worthy of study and, often, of preservation as the 'stately homes'. In particular the works of Mr Eric Mercer, Professor Maurice Barley, and Dr Ronald Brunskill have been of great value in drawing attention to the importance of the smaller house as a subject for serious study.

This book does not attempt to compete with the works of these authors, although it owes much to them. It is offered to owners and prospective purchasers of old houses, to those who live in or enjoy visiting old towns and villages or who, as members of Local Authorities, may have to decide on their future, and who want to find out more about the history of these buildings. It is concerned with changes in the way people have lived as well as with changes in architectural styles and fashions. If, by showing something of the interest to be found in the study of smaller houses, this book helps to encourage their more sympathetic treatment its purpose will have been achieved.

1
The story of your house: where to begin

When we look at an old house, whether as owners, prospective purchasers or visitors, one of the first questions we may find ourselves asking is 'How old is it?' Unfortunately, it is not often easy to give a precise answer to this question, especially in the case of small and medium sized houses.

With larger houses there may well be adequate documentary evidence for the dates of their first building and subsequent alterations, but this information is less often available for the smaller houses, whose first builders and subsequent owners were not sufficiently well off or important to have left behind them such records. Generally it may be said that the more recent the house, and the higher the status of its builders and subsequent owners, the more likely it is that documentary evidence of its age may exist.

The scientific methods of dating used by archaeologists are not normally applicable in these cases. Radio-carbon dating is not sufficiently accurate to be of much help here, and dendro-chronology — the dating of timber by examining its growth rings — is not fully developed for application in Great Britain. In any case, timbers in old buildings were often re-used from elsewhere.

When we consider the architectural evidence for the age of a house, we come up against the problem of architectural time-lag. Changes in architectural style did not take place at the same time over the whole country. In general, new ideas in Britain developed first in London and the South-east, the areas more closely in touch with the Continent and most influenced by the Court. From there they spread across the country, taking as long as a hundred years to reach the remoter areas of the North and West. In any given area, new ideas generally became established first in the towns, spreading out into the villages and rural areas. This applied particularly to the smaller and medium sized houses. The builders of the larger houses were more likely to be in touch with the latest architectural style than their less wealthy neighbours. Occasionally we may be fortunate

9

The story of your house: where to begin

enough to find an accurately dated building, and this can be used as a guide to date other similar houses in the area.

Another fact we must bear in mind is that very few houses survive today in the form in which they were first built. Inevitably they have been altered, enlarged, reconstructed, even completely rebuilt to suit the needs and tastes of successive owners. When we ask, 'How old is your house?' we may mean either the date of its first building, or the date of the major surviving work.

This may make our task harder, but no less interesting. Working out the history of successive alterations to a house can tell us much about its previous owners and their increasing or decreasing prosperity. Houses may move up or down in the social scale, and this is reflected in their architectural form. It may seem strange to say that architecture is not a static art, but in a very real sense this is true. Buildings have been changed, both in their form and in their use. Many old houses existing today were not built as dwellings but for other purposes, and have been converted and adapted for residential use. Even redundant churches are taking on a new lease of life as houses. Conversely, many houses have been converted for other uses, and this is a continuing process. In town centres old houses are still being converted to offices or shops, and in towns and rural areas large houses are being adapted for public and institutional use. All these factors have to be considered when working out the age and history of a house.

When we start on this task, we shall find that there are two sources of information: the documentary evidence which will include written information, maps and plans and the physical evidence which is both architectural and archaeological.

If we look first at the documentary evidence, the most obvious source would appear to be the deeds of the house, which may give some details of its building and subsequent reconstruction. Unfortunately these are sometimes rather disappointing, going back only to a comparatively recent date. If the earliest available deeds appear much more recent than the apparent age of the house, it is worth enquiring whether any earlier deeds have been deposited at the local Record Office. In many cases however, the early deeds have been destroyed.

It may be that no earlier deeds have existed if the house originally belonged to a large estate, as there may not have been any separate deeds for the property until it was sold. If, however, the whole estate has been sold in the past, the property in question may have been included in the deeds of the whole estate. If there are no conveyances, there may be leases of the property.

The story of your house: where to begin

In the case of estate and former estate properties there may be information in the estate records themselves. These vary considerably in their completeness and availability. Some have been deposited at the local Record Office and been well indexed. These may normally be inspected by arrangement with the Archivist. When the papers are still held by the estate, permission will have to be obtained to examine them. Estate surveys, valuations, leases and accounts relating to the building or repair of houses belonging to the estate can be most helpful here. Unfortunately these papers do not always identify the individual houses, often naming only the tenant concerned, but where properties can be identified on an estate map a useful start may be made.

After checking the deeds of the house, and any available estate records where applicable, the next step will probably be a visit to the local City or County Record Office, to see what information may be available there. It is now fairly common practice for early documents to be deposited at the local Record Office.

Here are some of the documentary sources which may be available at the local Record Office, or their whereabouts known to the Archivist:

Manorial Court Rolls

These are particularly valuable in the case of Copyhold houses, those where the tenancy was recorded by *copying* it in the Manorial Court Roll. They were usually held for three 'lives' or generations, not for a fixed term of years. This system of tenancy began in the Middle Ages and lasted until 1925, although by the nineteenth century it was generally being replaced by normal leases.

When a copyholder died the property normally passed to his heir (the next 'life'), and this is recorded in the court roll. In addition, a copyholder might surrender his tenement during his lifetime. This, and the admission of the new tenant, would also be recorded. The actual property was not necessarily named, but it is sometimes possible to identify it or its site from some item in the entry, which may also state when a tenement was first built or rebuilt by the tenant, with the permission of the lord of the manor. As mentioned on page 20, the Tithe Map and Apportionment gives the names of the owner and occupier of each property on which tithe had to be paid. If by chance the court roll continues until the date of the Tithe Map (generally about 1840), it may be possible to check the map against the court roll, and trace back the succession of tenants until an entry is found indicating the building or rebuilding of the house. One problem here is that

11

the early court rolls were in Latin, and this, in the script of the period, can be difficult for an amateur to decipher.

Glebe Terriers

In the case of present or former rectories and vicarages, and sometimes the glebe farms and other buildings belonging to the Church, the glebe terriers (inventories of the property of the benefice) may provide useful information. Sometimes the actual construction of the house is mentioned, and the fact that it had recently been built or enlarged. These terriers are normally kept at the Diocesan Registry or Record Office, but there may be copies in the local Record Office. Occasionally the terrier may include a plan or drawing of the house, sometimes with the date of the building or alteration.

Cathedral Records

In the cathedral cities the cathedral bodies, generally the Dean and Chapter, owned property, and their records may give useful information. The leases may incorporate descriptions of houses, and even plans. These records, like the glebe terriers, are normally to be found in the Diocesan Registry.

Borough Records

Both in the cathedral cities and in other old towns information may be obtained from the Borough Records. Some of the boroughs owned a considerable amount of property, and leases, rentals and other records may still exist from the Tudor period, and even earlier. These records sometimes give dates of the building of houses and cottages, and as with the cathedral records, may include plans. As mentioned previously, records dating from before the seventeenth century are likely to be in Latin.

For more recent buildings – those of the eighteenth and nineteenth centuries – the Borough Records may be even more helpful as the authorities began to assume responsibility for the control and supervision of building development. Surveys of existing housing, and plans of proposed new housing may all be found here, although unfortunately some of this evidence has disappeared in the successive reorganisations of Local Government. Some of the earlier documents are now deposited at the local Record Office.

The story of your house: where to begin

The Town Directories, dating back in some instances to the eighteenth century, may give further information, as may Burgess Rolls, Rate Books, the Gas and Water Companies' account books, and the Census Records. Most of these may be found in the local Record Office, or their whereabouts known to the Archivist. British census records are held at the Land Registry Building, Portugal Street, London, but there may be copies in the local Record Office.

Wills and Probate Inventories

Other possible sources of information are Wills and Probate Inventories. The wills of all but the most wealthy were generally proved in the local ecclesiastical courts, and these, and probate inventories if they have survived, are probably kept in the Diocesan Registry or the County Record Office. In some cases wills may be found dating back to the medieval period, and these sometimes include a description of the house of the deceased.

Probate Inventories, giving a list of all the possessions of the deceased, provided that their total value was at least £5, were required to be made under an Act of Parliament of 1529, and continued to be made until the nineteenth century. These inventories were made by friends and neighbours of the deceased, and sometimes mention the separate rooms of the house, giving an indication of its size and the use made of the various rooms as indicated by their contents. These inventories, like the wills, were prepared for the church authorities. Generally, the earlier the inventory, the more detailed it is likely to be.

Here again, individual houses are not often named, but the burial entry in the Parish Register may sometimes give the name of the house, particularly if it is a farm, occupied by the deceased.

Tax Returns

Early tax returns, also possibly available at the local Record Office, may be helpful, if one can identify the house from them. This can normally only be done if the name of the occupier at the time is known. The Hearth Tax, in operation from 1662 to 1685, listed the number of hearths in the house, and this may be compared with the present number, helping to show whether the house has been enlarged or reduced in size. This also shows the social status of the house: only the more important rooms were heated at this period.

13

An eighteenth-century Probate Inventory tells us quite a lot about the deceased's house.

Maps and Plans

In addition to written records we may be helped by early maps and plans. Here again the local Record Office or the local museum will probably be the best starting point. Some maps were produced by the large estates, and may be studied in conjunction with the estate records, helping to identify

EAST LULWORTH OLD INCLOSURES.

JOHN SAXEY FARM.

No.		A.	R.	P.
32	Homeftall	0	1	39
111	Higher Millbourn	6	3	3
114	Cherry's Clofe	3	3	17
115	Lower Millbourn	2	0	14
117	Ford's Clofe	3	3	25
118	Broad Clofe	7	2	7
121	Clofe	2	0	22
122	Clofe	2	0	1
123	Baker's under Hill Clofe	6	2	18
131	Cherry's Clofe	3	0	17
132	Cherry's Cow-Leaze	4	3	15
133	Ford's Cow-Leaze	4	0	11
234	Ford's Mead	3	1	3
241	Clofe	3	1	23
242	Clofe	2	1	34
		56	2	10

IN HAND.

No.		A.	R.	P.
11	Clofe	6	0	27
26	Crofs Clofe	3	2	24
27	Baker's Clofe	2	3	22
53	Homeftall and Clofe adjoining	1	0	19
72	Clofe	1	0	20
		1	7	2	5
74	Newnhams	2	4	0	32
		3	6	0	9
110	Elme's Clofe	3	0	31
130	Clofe	2	2	1
253	Demefnes of the Cattle	39	2	38
		43	0	28

WOODS IN HAND.

No.		A.	R.	P.
152	Bowling-Green Wood	21	0	23
147	Needy Pit Nurfery	2	0	7
148	Nurfery	1	2	8
149	Park Wood	26	1	9
150	Park Wood	37	0	29
151	Concygar Wood	14	1	19
		102	2	15

JAMES SEYMOUR.

No.		A.	R.	P.
5	Homeftall and Clofe adjoining	1	0	14
105	Clofe	1	2	9
120	Clofe	1	0	36
		3	3	19

ROBERT WOOLFRY.

No.		A.	R.	P.
6	Clofe	1	0	7
12	Houfe and Garden	0	0	10
19	Homeftall and Clofe adjoining	0	3	35
		2	0	12

HESTER SEYMOUR.

No.		A.	R.	P.
7	Clofe	1	0	28
24	Homeftall	0	1	2
49	Garden	0	0	16
50	Homeftall and Clofe adjoining	1	2	25
107	Tramel Clofe	0	1	29
140	Peaked Mead	1	2	32
		5	1	12

ROBERT MILLER.

No.		A.	R.	P.
9	Houfe and Garden	0	0	13
25	Homeftall and Clofe adjoining	0	3	18
108	Clofe	1	2	12
109	Clofe	1	3	6
		4	1	9

WILLIAM HATCHARD, COPYHOLD.

No.		A.	R.	P.
10	Homeftall and Clofe adjoining	1	1	37
XIII	Homeftall, Clofe, and a Cottage	3	2	17
119	Clofe	3	3	34
125	Long Clofe	3	3	37
126	Long Clofe	2	1	39
127	Baker's Brook Clofe	2	3	17
128	Brook Clofe	4	3	19
129	Baker's Brook Clofe	2	1	34
		26	2	25

SARAH SEYMOUR.

No.		A.	R.	P.
33	Homeftall and Clofe adjoining	0	2	21
34	Clofe	1	3	39
35	Clofe	1	0	28
135	Clofe	2	1	25
136	Clofe	2	0	21
		8	1	5

GRACE KEAT.

No.		A.	R.	P.
61	Homeftall and Clofe adjoining	1	1	0
62	Home Clofe	2	0	22
64	Wilkthir's Peak Clofe	2	1	1
112	Higher Marley	2	0	32
113	Lower Marley	2	3	38
124	Oakley Wood Clofe	6	0	36
		17	0	8

JOHN CULL.

No.		A.	R.	P.
106	Brand Clofe	3	0	36

JOSEPH GARLAND, COPYHOLD.

No.		A.	R.	P.
116	Clofe	1	0	0

COTTAGES.

No.		A.	R.	P.
2	Mary Seymour Houfe and Garden	0	0	6
3	Sarah Penny Houfe and Houfe	0	1	18
85	Ditto two Gardens and Houfe	0	0	20
4	Thomas Hames Houfe, Yard and Garden	0	0	34
8	Elizabeth Bartlet Houfe and Garden	0	0	14
15	John Ford Houfe and Garden	0	1	10
16	John Gold, Senior, Houfe and Garden	0	0	13
17	Jonathan Battrick Houfe and Garden	0	0	13
18	John Baker Houfe and Garden	0	0	38
20	Mary Woolfry Houfe and Garden	0	0	19
21	George Swier Houfe and Garden	0	1	11
22	John Tuexbury Garden	0	0	27
23	Ditto Houfe and Garden	0	0	10
28	Thomas Baker Houfe and Garden	0	0	32
29	Robert Hunt Houfe and Garden	0	0	28
31	Mary Penny Houfe and Garden	0	0	20
36	Mary Flowers Houfe and Garden	0	0	8
38	Ditto Houfe and Garden	0	0	2
39	Richard Keat Houfe and Garden	0	0	2
39	Ditto a Garden	0	0	6
40	Ditto a Garden	0	0	19
42	Jofeph Keat Houfe and Garden	0	0	16
44	Ditto a Garden	0	0	13
41	William Snook Houfe and Garden	0	0	25
45	Barnard Eveleigh Garden	0	0	20
48	Ditto Houfe and Garden	0	0	27
93	Ditto Houfe and Garden	0	0	20
57	Sarah World Garden	0	0	12
69	John World Houfe and Garden	0	0	19
70	Judith Cockram Houfe and Garden	0	1	2
73	Thomas Tuexbury Houfe and Garden	0	1	34
75	George Hunt Houfe and Garden	0	0	9
76	John Haxt Houfe and Garden	0	0	4
77	John Bithey Houfe and Garden	0	0	7
79	Ditto a Garden	0	0	16
78	James Slade Houfe and Garden	0	0	16
80	Robert Galton Houfe and Garden	0	0	13
81	William Adams Houfe and Garden	0	0	11
82	David Grant Houfe and Garden	0	0	3
88	Ditto Stable and Garden	0	0	1
100	Ditto a Clofe	0	0	24
83	Christopher Baker Houfe and Garden	0	0	20
84	Jofeph Adams Houfe and Garden	0	0	12
86	Ditto a Garden	0	0	12
87	Ditto a Garden	0	0	6
89	Hannah Slade Houfe and Garden	0	1	12
90	Elizabeth Champ Houfe and Garden	0	1	18
91	John Hunt Houfe and Garden	0	0	30
92	William Penny Houfe and Garden	0	0	31
95	Ditto a Garden	0	0	16
98	Widow of Henry Penny Houfe and Garden	0	1	10
97	Ditto a Garden	0	0	6
96	Charles Ricketts Houfe and Garden	0	1	12
99	Mofes Roberts Houfe and Garden	0	1	18
99	John Wilton Garden	0	1	15
101	Ditto Houfe and Garden	0	0	27
102	Thomas and Jofeph Slade a Garden			
		7	3	17

Extract from an Estate Survey at East Lulworth, Dorset, c 1768, indicating old and new enclosures with names of the freeholders and tenants, as shown on the map overleaf.

actual houses. Of course, the fact that a house is shown on an early map does not necessarily mean that it is the same building as now exists, but it may indicate that a house which appears comparatively recent is a refacing or remodelling of a much earlier structure, and more worthy of investigation than at first appears.

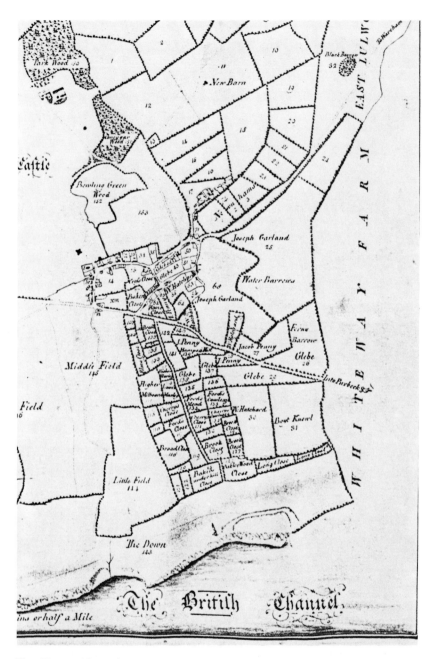

The Estate Map of East Lulworth, c 1768, shows the position of the
tenancies listed on the previous page.

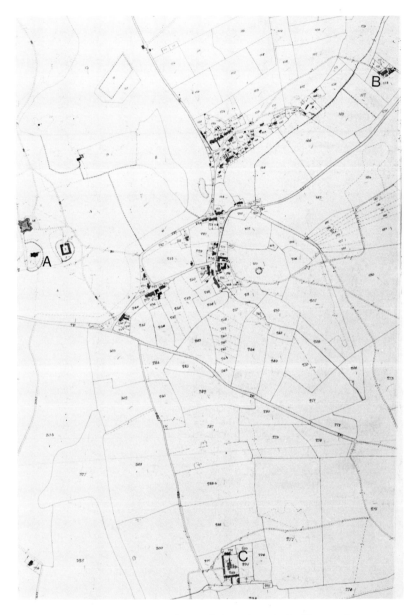

Tithe map of the same area of East Lulworth, c 1840. The north-west part of the village has been demolished and the land incorporated into the park of the castle, leaving the church (A) isolated. Additional estate cottages have been built in the north-east part of the village, and new farms indicated at B and C have been built in the enclosed fields away from the original village centre.

17

The 1902 Ordnance Survey Map of East Lulworth, and a modern aerial photograph. Both show little development since the early nineteenth century, probably because the village has remained in the ownership of one estate.

18

19

The story of your house: where to begin

The Tithe Map

For many parishes the Tithe Map of about 1840 survives, this having been prepared when the Parish tithes were commuted for a fixed annual charge on each property. There is sometimes one of similar or earlier date accompanying an Enclosure Award. The larger scale Ordnance Survey maps were being produced from about 1850. Where more than one early map survives for a parish or town, it may be possible to see when the house we are studying first appears. The Tithe Apportionment accompanying the Tithe Map will also give the names of the owner and occupier of each house and plot of land at that date, and may tell us something of the status of both these persons, as well as the amount of land associated with the house. As stated earlier, if the court roll for the parish also exists, covering the date of the Tithe Map, it may be possible to trace back the occupants of the house, perhaps to the date of its first building. If we are exceptionally lucky, we may also be able to study the wills and inventories of these occupants, giving an indication of any changes in the size of the house over this period.

Some early maps actually show little drawings of the houses, rather than indicating them simply as blocks. While making allowance for artistic licence, these often help to show whether the house marked on the map is the one shown today or its predecessor. The size of the house thus shown, and the number of chimneys, windows, etc. also gives some idea of its social status.

In addition to these sources the Archivist will probably be able to suggest other possible sources of information, which could include some of the following:

Local County Histories
Town and County Guide Books (These should be used with care – some may have been written by enthusiastic but none too knowledgeable amateurs.)
Local Museum collections
Transactions of local Historical Societies
The Local Collection in the Public Library

Further sources

Mention must be made of two 'official' and at first sight authoritative sources of information. These are the Lists of Buildings of Special Architectural or Historic Interest, prepared by the Department of Culture,

The story of your house: where to begin

Media and Sport and the Survey of the Royal Commission on Historical Monuments. The Department Lists (about which more details are given in Chapter 11), cover the whole of Britain, and may be inspected at the County and District Council Offices. The Survey of the Royal Commission on Historical Monuments is far from complete, at present covering only certain counties.

Although the Department Lists are useful as a starting point, the datings shown in them cannot necessarily be assumed to be accurate. Often the dating given is based on a superficial external inspection only, and as we shall see, this may be much later than the actual date of the structure. Houses were often refaced to reflect the latest architectural fashion. It is also worth stressing here that the description given in these Lists are simply intended to identify the building, and to indicate that it is of sufficient historical or architectural interest to merit preservation. Such descriptions are not intended to be exhaustive, or even to include all the significant features of the building.

The Survey of the Royal Commission on Historical Monuments is being prepared in more detail, and in some cases plans of houses are included. Here again, however, particularly in the case of smaller houses, the entries are not always entirely accurate or complete. In addition, there is the Survey of London, started by the former London County and Greater London Councils and being continued by the Royal Commission on Historical Monuments. This is being done most thoroughly, and is a very useful document for those areas of London which have been completed.

Apart from all these official and legal sources of information, we should not neglect literary sources. Contemporary travellers' accounts, diaries and letters may all throw light on the existence and condition of houses and other buildings, as may early drawings and prints and old photographs. The local Public Library will probably be able to supply a list of publications relating to the area. Local newspapers may well contain descriptions of houses, as well as sale particulars. Here again, the Library or the Record Office may have copies of the local newspapers dating back a century or more.

The name of the house, if it can be traced back as authentic over a considerable period, may help in our researches. It may for instance commemorate the name of a former owner or occupier, but we must not be led astray by recent names given for prestige or romantic reasons. Many houses today are known as 'Manors' or 'Priories' with no historical justification.

**A date stone with the name of
the owner has additional value**

When we come to consider the physical evidence for dating a house, it falls under two headings, architectural and archaeological. While we cannot draw a fine dividing line between these, in general the architectural evidence concerns the house as it is today, and the archaeological evidence concerns any relics of an earlier building on the site, or parts of the building which have been destroyed or changed in the course of successive alterations.

One feature which might be said to combine both documentary and physical evidence is the date-stone often found in an old house over the front door, on a chimney stack or on an external wall. Unfortunately, such stones, although often of considerable help, cannot be taken as firm evidence for the date of the building. They may indicate a date of repair, a major or minor reconstruction, or commemorate the marriage of a former owner. Indeed it is not unknown for date-stones to be moved from one building to another. Even if we discount the possibility of a deliberate fake (or a practical joke) these date stones must always be considered in conjunction with other evidence. A date is more likely to be authentic if it is cut on a structural feature such as a door or fireplace lintel, rather than on a separate stone which could more easily have been moved from elsewhere.

The potential value of a date-stone increases when it is accompanied by the name of the initials of the presumed owner, sometimes with those of his wife. A search in the Parish Registers of Baptisms, Marriages and Burials may identify the owner. These Registers may still be in the church, or have been deposited in the local Record Office. If the date commemorates a marriage, this event may have coincided with the building or improvement of the house. Having thus traced the owner at a particular date, it may be possible to find his will and probate inventory (assuming

**Fire insurance plaque
on the side of a house**

that he was still living in the same house when he died). This could throw further light on the size and status of the house at that date. From this point, too, it may be possible to trace back earlier occupants through deeds, leases or entries in the court roll.

Another rather similar item which may help in dating a house is the fire insurance plaque sometimes found on an external wall. These plaques date from the period when each Insurance Company maintained its own fire brigade, which only attended fires affecting the properties insured by that company. Each plaque will probably have a number – that of the policy – and the records of the Company (or its successor if it has been amalgamated with others) should provide useful information. There may be a description of the house as insured at that date and subsequently, providing a record of alterations. In the nineteenth century some insurance companies prepared plans of their insured houses and these, compared with the present form of the house, will be a useful guide to subsequent alterations. For this reason it is always unfortunate when these insurance plaques are removed from their original sites to be sold as antiques, or even fixed to other buildings.

If our researches into the documentary evidence have revealed the date of the house, and confirmed that the surviving building is substantially of that date, we shall have been very fortunate indeed and, using the architectural style of the house as a guide, we can proceed to date other similar houses in the area with reasonable accuracy. It is far more likely, however, that the evidence will be inconclusive, perhaps indicating possible dates which we shall have to try to corroborate from the structure of the house.

This will be detailed in later chapters, but at this stage I should like to

23

The story of your house: where to begin

stress that any old house is, apart from any other merits it may have, a valuable historical record – a three-dimensional document. Today most people appreciate the value of historic documents and the importance of their preservation, interpretation and recording. The practice of cutting up old wills, deeds and indentures to make lampshades, and even their deliberate destruction is now, we hope, rare. It is less commonly appreciated that a historic building deserves equal care. This applies to smaller houses as well as to stately homes, for history is not just made up of famous people.

Of course, houses, if they are to survive as homes, may have to be adapted for life today – indeed this has been a continuing process. As the number of old houses decreases, however, so the value of unspoiled examples is increasing, as is the need for care in their treatment. Far too many of the smaller old houses have been spoiled, and their historic value lost, by insensitive modernisation, often due to a lack of knowledge of their significance. Simply maintaining a superficial prettiness is poor compensation for the loss of all historical authenticity. We often hear the phrase: 'I haven't altered it outside', or, 'at the front'. As we shall see later, the two most important elements in an old house, from the point of view of its historic significance, are probably the plan form and the roof structure. If, for the reasons already stated, it is difficult to put a precise date to a small house, the task becomes impossible when the house has been completely gutted internally, or has had its history falsified by the introduction of bogus period features.

Having given this warning it may seem paradoxical to say that the carrying out of repairs and alterations may provide a good opportunity to find out more about the history of a house. It is often during the removal of plaster from walls, for instance, that evidence of earlier doors and windows comes to light, and excavation for drains may reveal foundations of earlier walls and even pottery, coins and other finds, all of which can help in the dating of the house.

It would be unreasonable and useless to say that old houses should never be altered today. If we care about the house we should not start work without first making as careful a survey as possible, recording all surviving features, and finding out all we can about its history and development. Then, as the work proceeds, there should be continuous supervision and observation in case new evidence comes to light. Any pottery or other objects found should be saved, and the place where they were found recorded. The local museum will probably be able to help in dating any finds.

The gable wall of an earlier house, later demolished, can clearly be seen as part of the end wall of Rowley's House, Shrewsbury.

Evidence of former doors and
windows revealed during alterations

If any early features are uncovered, such as door and window openings, fireplaces and associated features such as bread ovens and curing chambers, moulded or carved ceiling beams, work should stop until these have been examined and recorded. It may be desirable to alter the plans to enable such features to be preserved. Work on an old house should only be entrusted to a builder who can be relied upon to stop work and report such findings.

Particular care should be taken when repairs or alterations are carried out on old roofs. If some of the timbers are defective and the roof is out of true, there will be a great temptation to renew the roof completely, thus destroying much important evidence. It may be that, unless there is access to the roof space, nothing will be known about the age or construction of the roof until work starts. An inspection of the roof may provide the final confirmation that the house was originally of the open hall form as well as valuable evidence of later alterations and additions. No old roof timbers should be removed until a full survey has been carried out, and the structure recorded by drawings and photographs.

In trying to work out the age and history of a house the documentary and the physical evidence are complementary. Neither is likely on its own to tell the complete story, but if we are fortunate and prepared to spend time and trouble, the two can be pieced together to tell us a great deal about the house we are studying, the successive changes in its status, and the way of life of its occupants.

Crown post roof revealed during repairs to St Catherine's Cottage, Shorne, Kent.

2
Historical development of the house: Medieval foundations

The house is, of course, the most basic and essential of buildings, and the story of its development is a continuous one, from the primitive shelters of prehistoric times to the houses of our own day. Most towns and villages contain houses of many different periods, and often the houses themselves incorporate work of more than one period. Before we can start to work out the story of our house we must know something of the development of domestic architecture.

Although in this book we are looking primarily at the smaller and medium sized house and cottage, we must look first at the early development of the larger and more sophisticated type of house – the house of the comparatively well off. This is for two reasons. First, it is only the houses of this class which have survived from the early medieval period. Our knowledge of peasant and artisan houses of this date comes from archaeological excavation, and sometimes indirectly from written evidence. Second, the design of the smaller houses and cottages was to some extent influenced by that of the larger houses. New ideas gradually filtered down the social scale.

By the end of the medieval period there had evolved what we might call the typical manor house plan. The term 'Manor' is not strictly architectural but legal, and perhaps its most accurate use today is by the police to describe the area covered by a particular Station! This plan, however, which had a considerable influence on that of the smaller house, was developed from two main early types, while a third rather specialised type had less direct influence, although it was sometimes combined with the other two.

The first basic house type, dating back at least to the time of the Norman conquest, was the first-floor hall, as shown in fig. 1. In this context, the word hall means the principal living area, not the entrance vestibule it eventually became. These houses were normally of two storeys, of which the ground storey was used for storage or service rooms,

Ground floor used for storage or services

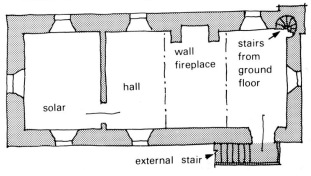

Fig. 1 **A first-floor hall**

The Jew's House, Lincoln. A Norman first-floor hall house with living accommodation above the shop and stores.

29

Historical development:

sometimes vaulted in stone for security and fire protection. The first floor contained a large general purpose living room – the hall – and usually a smaller private room for the owner, known as the solar (literally the 'room above the floor') which was probably primarily a sleeping room.

The hall was normally approached by an external staircase and heated by a wall fireplace, while the solar was often unheated. Examples of this type of house have survived from the twelfth century and, not surprisingly, the surviving examples are nearly all of stone, although many must have been built of timber, the usual material for all but the most wealthy at this time. They are found both in towns and in rural areas, and continued to be built into the fifteenth century. In towns this plan had the advantage of saving space; the shop, workshop, or other business areas would be on the ground floor, with the living areas above. In rural areas, this form of house was probably favoured for purposes of defence.

Generally, the first-floor hall houses are not large. A number are still inhabited, and it is possible that more examples remain to be discovered, their original form obscured by later alterations. After the fourteenth century, when the need for defence was less pressing, first-floor hall houses were less common, although they continued to be built, or were revived, for a particular purpose, as will be seen later.

The second basic house type was the aisled-hall (fig. 2). Archaeological evidence for these buildings shows that they were being built in Saxon

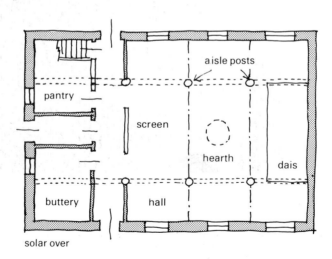

Fig. 2 **An aisled-hall**   Scale of feet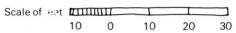

10   0   10   20   30

Lodge Farm, Pamphill, Wimborne, Dorset. The exterior of this small house presented rather an unprepossessing picture, as shown above. Removal of the rendering, however, revealed a number of medieval windows, which have now been restored (top). The building proved to be a late medieval first-floor hall house, described in more detail overleaf.

31

Historical development:

Lodge Farm dates from the late fourteenth or early fifteenth century. Situated in the outer area of Cranborne Chase it may have originated as a hunting lodge (it is named The Lodge on a seventeenth-century map of the Chase). The ground floor (*fig. 4a*) was probably used as service or store rooms, or as subsidiary living accommodation.

FRONT ELEVATION

Fig. 3

Fig. 4b

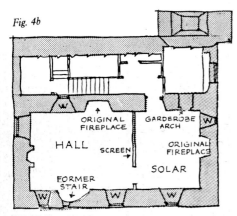

FIRST FLOOR.   W = ORIGINAL WINDOW

Above this (*fig. 4b*) is a two-bay hall, open to the roof, with a single-bay solar adjoining it. The hall was heated by a fireplace in the rear wall, and was approached by a spiral stair partly recessed into the front wall. A garderobe led off the solar, and the entrance arch to this and part of the walling survive. The solar also had a fireplace. The roof is of arch-braced collar form, with wind bracing and with moulded wall plates in the solar, which may always have been ceiled.

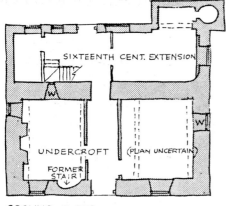

GROUND FLOOR

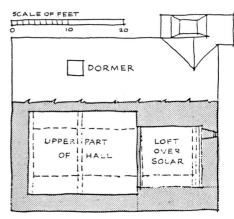

ATTIC LEVEL

Fig. 4a   *Fig. 4c*

32

Medieval foundations

In the late sixteenth or early seventeenth century the hall was floored over and a lean-to kitchen added at the rear, removing the upper part of the garderobe (see left). Chimneys were inserted in the end gable walls to heat the ground-floor rooms, and both the original fireplaces were blocked, a new end fireplace being inserted in the hall. The house may have become a farmhouse at this time, using the ground-floor rooms for the main living accommodation.

The hall, used as a bedroom, was reduced in size by re-siting the partition between it and the solar. Some of the medieval windows were built up and others had part or all of their tracery removed. Internally, however, many original features survived. The hall has now been opened up by removing the later ceiling, revealing the original roof (see above), and the original first-floor plan restored. The medieval windows have been opened up and their tracery restored (left).

33

times. Indeed, some early Roman villas were of this form, although it would be difficult to prove any real continuity. Some of these early aisled-halls were quite large, and they may have been used as assembly places for the community as well as private houses. Although some surviving examples are stone built, for example the halls of Oakham and Winchester Castles, most of them were probably of timber and must have resembled large barns.

The adoption of this plan enabled a wide-span building to be roofed fairly simply, although the aisle posts were an obstruction. In the earliest period the hall probably housed the owner's animals as well as himself, his family and servants. The removal of the animals to a separate byre, possibly still attached to the house, was a step forward, as was the separation of a room at one end of the hall for the private use of the owner. This might be at ground floor level, or raised on an undercroft or cellar used for storage, both storeys being accommodated within the total height of the hall. Nearer the other end of the hall there were generally two doors facing each other in the long walls, with a screen between them to protect the hall from draughts. Beyond this area were the service rooms, the pantry for storing food and the buttery for keeping drink. In the earliest period these may have been lean-to structures of lighter construction than the hall itself, but they were eventually incorporated into the main structure, sometimes with the solar or private room above them rather than at the 'upper' end of the hall.

The hall was heated by an open fire in the centre, with a louvre in the roof above it to allow the smoke to escape. The kitchen was an independent detached structure separated from the hall to reduce the risk of fire, and was approached by a passage between the pantry and the buttery.

At the upper end of the hall, furthest from the doors and screen, there was often a raised platform or dais for the high table of the owner. Windows at this early period would probably have been unglazed, fitted with shutters or lattices. The floor was usually of beaten earth, covered with rushes.

A number of aisled-hall houses of timber construction and medium size have survived from the late medieval period, most of them in East Anglia (fig. 5). In nearly all cases an intermediate floor has been inserted in the hall, and the aisle posts have been incorporated in later partitions, so that the original form of the house is not apparent. The aisled-hall house is also found in Yorkshire, particularly in the Halifax area. Here the external walls have generally been rebuilt in stone at a later date, again obscuring the original form of the house.

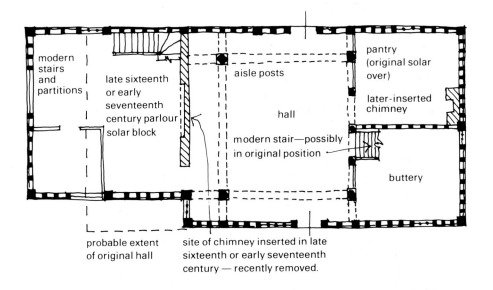

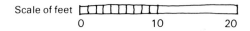

Scale of feet

0   10   20

Fig. 5 **Purton Green Farm House, Stansfield, Suffolk. This house, of modest size, is an important surviving example of a timber-framed aisled-hall house, dating from the mid thirteenth century. It consisted originally of a two-bay hall with a central truss, open to the roof, and a pantry/buttery block with a chamber over at one end. The upper end of the hall was rebuilt and extended in the late sixteenth or early seventeenth century to provide a new parlour/solar block. At about the same time the hall was floored over, and a chimney stack inserted at the upper end. There is no evidence for the existence or otherwise of an earlier two-storeyed block at this end, and the house may originally have been of the end hall form, with the solar above the service rooms.**

The aisle posts must have been in the way, and eventually the builders learnt to construct a roof over the whole of the hall without the need for these intermediate supports. The development of the open timber roof, culminating in the hammer-beam design, is a subject for study on its own, but basically the problem was to design a roof without internal obstructions which would not exert an undue amount of outward thrust on the external walls.

This problem was sometimes solved by the use of 'base crucks', large curved timbers which transferred the weight of the roof outwards and down the walls to the ground, thus avoiding outward thrust at eaves level, and the consequent danger of overturning the walls. Even after the

Purton Green Farm, Stansfield, Suffolk.

The roof construction is of particular interest; there are no principal rafters, purlins, or ridge piece. The structure is strengthened on the lines of the aisle posts by parallel bracing rafters. This form of construction perhaps evolved into the trussed rafter and crown-post roof typical of the later Middle Ages, particularly in the south and east of Britain.

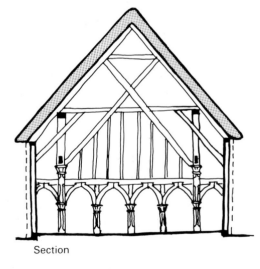

Section

Purton Green Farm, Stansfield, Suffolk.
Interior of the hall looking towards the service rooms, showing an aisle post incorporated in the partition.

Purton Green Farm must have been built for a wealthy farmer, but over the centuries it was divided into tenements, and eventually became derelict. In 1969 it was acquired by the Landmark Trust, and has since been renovated. The hall has been opened up, and modern living accommodation provided in the parlour/solar block. The smoke-blackened timbers of the hall roof show that the house was originally heated by an open hearth.

builders had learnt to construct these wide-span roofs, we find aisle posts surviving in the truss containing the screen at the lower end of the hall, where they created no obstruction. This truss, incorporating aisle posts and acting as a frame for the screen, was known as a spere truss. It is a feature most often found in the Midlands and northern part of Britain.

With the disappearance of the aisle posts, and the increasing use of stone for the walls, at least in the larger houses, this type of house (i.e. the ground-floor hall) began to supersede the first-floor hall, particularly as the need for defensive structures lessened. The fully developed later medieval manor house (fig. 6) was generally of the following form:

The hall, open to the roof and equivalent to two storeys in height, was the dominant feature architecturally, just as it was the social hub of the house. It might be of two, three, four or more bays in length – the bay being the space between two roof trusses – depending on the status of the

37

Historical development:

Lower Brockhampton, Hereford and Worcestershire. An unaisled hall house showing the aisle posts retained in the spere truss. A ladder-type stair gives access to the gallery above the screens passage.

owner. At the lower end were the entrance doors, facing each other in each of the long sides, with a wooden screen linking the doors to protect the hall from draughts and forming an internal passage known as the 'screens passage'. In later examples the screen is treated as a decorative feature, and sometimes has a gallery above it, extending over the passage.

Beyond the screens passage were the service rooms, the pantry and the buttery, and sometimes there was a passage between them leading to a kitchen, which might still be a detached structure. At the opposite end of the hall was a raised platform or dais for the high table. This end of the hall was often lit by a larger window, sometimes in the form of a bay or 'oriel'. At this upper end of the hall a door led to a withdrawing room or parlour for the owner. Both the parlour and the service rooms were normally ceiled at first-floor level, with rooms over them within the height of the hall: the solar or principal bedroom over the parlour, and either another bedroom or store rooms over the pantry and buttery. The hall was still generally heated by an open hearth, with a smoke louvre in the roof above it, although in later examples this was often replaced by a wall fireplace. There were sometimes porches to one or both of the outer doors to the hall. This layout may still be seen in the dining halls of some of the Oxford and Cambridge colleges.

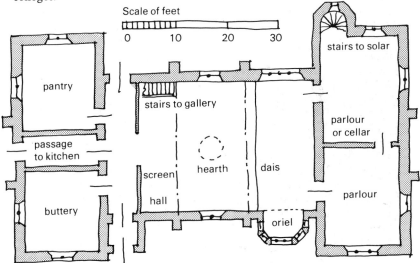

Fig. 6 **Typical later medieval manor house plan. This plan, evolved from the aisled-hall, had largely superseded the first-floor hall plan by the late fourteenth century. It was to influence the design of smaller houses from this period to the late seventeenth century.**

Sometimes the parlour and pantry blocks were roofed separately from the hall, at right angles to it, forming projecting wings. All these wings were only one room deep, because of the limitations of the roof construction, and rooms were generally inter-communicating, without corridors. By the later Middle Ages window glass had become more common in the larger houses, and this must have added considerably to their comfort. Internal walls were normally plastered, often with painted decoration. Tapestries and wood panelling, originally introduced for greater warmth, also provided opportunities for decorative treatment. Artificial lighting was provided by candles, rush lights, or cresset-type lamps with a wick floating in oil.

Apart from the first-floor hall and the aisled-hall, there was a third early medieval house type which had some influence on later development. This was the tower house, almost certainly defensive in origin, and probably derived from the square keep of the early Norman castles. Sometimes the tower comprised the whole house, with storage rooms on the ground floor and living accommodation above it. In other examples the solar block of a ground or first-floor hall was carried up as a tower. These tower houses were more common in areas where defence was a prime consideration, particularly near the Scottish borders. Here houses of this type continued to be built and occupied until the union of Scotland with England under the Stuarts.

Towards the end of the medieval period, by the later fifteenth century, we find some houses being built with a hall only one storey high; that is, of two storeys throughout. Above the hall was another room, apparently of equal importance to it. This type of house may be considered a revival, or possibly a continuation, of the first-floor hall type. It is not normally found in the largest houses, where the great open hall was still a dominant feature. These late medieval two-storeyed houses are generally of medium size, and in many cases seem to have been built by the Church. They may be Rectories, houses of Chantry priests or Monastic Granges, and they generally had a simple rectangular plan, the projecting wings at each end having been absorbed into the main block.

So far we have been looking at the larger houses, those built by the comparatively wealthy, but these formed only a small part of the total housing stock of the Middle Ages. The great majority of houses were built for humbler people, yeomen, peasants, and artisans. There is no absolute line dividing the two categories of house; in particular, it is often difficult to distinguish the small manor house from the large farmhouse. This reflects the social flexibility of English society. People could move from

The Chantry, Trent, Dorset. A fifteenth century two-storeyed house, probably built as a priest's house.

one class to another, by success in farming, in business or in marriage, and this is shown in their homes. In general, the development of the smaller houses followed that of the larger houses, on a simpler scale and after a time-lag that was often considerable, especially in remote country areas.

Smaller Houses

Very few small houses or cottages have survived from before the Tudor period. In spite of estate agents' descriptions of 'thirteenth-century cottages', few yeomen, husbandmen, artisans or labourers could afford to build houses of any permanence before the late fifteenth or early sixteenth centuries. Excavations on the sites of deserted medieval villages show that small houses were often rebuilt in each generation. A house was not expected to last more than a lifetime.

As these houses have not survived, apart from their foundations, evidence for their form is archaeological only, and from this evidence it appears that the earliest huts were basically of two forms: circular and

41

Historical development: Medieval foundations

rectangular. The circular hut was built rather like a wigwam, with pole rafters converging at a central apex forming a conical shape. In the earliest examples the poles seem to have been sunk straight into the ground, but later they were raised on low walls of turf, earth or stone, to give improved headroom. Sometimes the floor was dug out below ground level, for the same purpose. With the rectangular huts, the pole rafters were supported on a longitudinal ridge pole, in turn supported by vertical posts at each end and at intervals along the length of the hut as required. As with the circular huts, the floor might be sunk, and the rafter feet, at first sunk into the ground, were later raised on low walls.

The two forms of hut may be compared to the bell tent and the ridge tent. The circular form was eventually superseded by the more convenient rectangular form. The roofs were covered with turf, heather or straw. The simplest rectangular hut consisted of one all-purpose room, but from an early date there is evidence of the hut being divided into two parts, one for the owner and his family and the other for his animals. There may have been no structural division between the two sections, the separation being marked only by opposed doors in the centre of each of the long walls, forming or suggesting a through-passage. This is the origin of the long-house plan. The house part was heated by a central hearth, the smoke finding its way out through a hole in the roof.

Cruck construction

Clearly, one great disadvantage of these early huts was the lack of headroom. With the simple coupled roof construction it was difficult to increase the height of the walls, since the thrust from the roof would tend to overturn them. The development of the cruck truss roof was a great improvement. Instead of the simple inclined pole rafters, and the ridge pole supported on vertical posts, the roof was formed with crucks – pairs of naturally curved timbers of substantial section, fixed together at the apex – giving a profile something like that of an upturned boat. This in itself gave more space inside the house, but a further improvement was made by fixing a horizontal tie-beam across the pair of crucks, and allowing it to project beyond them. The tie-beams supported horizontal wall plates running the length of the building, and these in turn supported the feet of the rafters which met at a ridge piece carried on the apexes of the crucks (fig. 7).

The whole roof was thus supported on the pairs of crucks, which were spaced between twelve and sixteen feet apart, the space between each pair

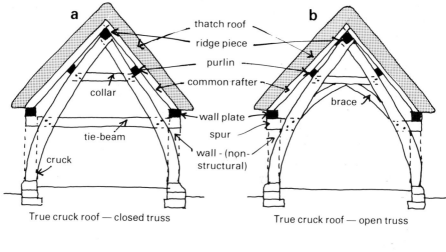

a

thatch roof
ridge piece
purlin
common rafter
collar
wall plate
tie-beam
spur
cruck
wall - (non-structural)

True cruck roof — closed truss

b

brace

True cruck roof — open truss

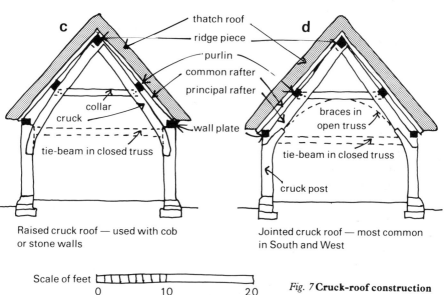

c

thatch roof
ridge piece
purlin
common rafter
principal rafter
collar
cruck
wall plate
tie-beam in closed truss

Raised cruck roof — used with cob or stone walls

d

braces in open truss
tie-beam in closed truss
cruck post

Jointed cruck roof — most common in South and West

Scale of feet

0   10   20

Fig. 7 **Cruck-roof construction**

being known as a bay. Walls could now be built, of timber-framing, stone or cob, and these had only to support their own weight. They did not have to resist any thrust from the roof. A similar principle may be seen in the portal frames of steel or concrete used for some agricultural and industrial buildings today. Incidentally, the presence of these curved crucks in a

43

house often gives rise to the belief that the house was built with old ships' timbers.

We now have a simple form of house, such as might be occupied by the medieval peasant farmer. There would be, perhaps, two bays for the living area, with another one or two bays forming the byre for the animals, with a through-passage or opposed doorways between them. In the living area at the end furthest from the byre, part might be partitioned off to form an inner room, and this might be lofted over within the height of the main building, for a sleeping space or for storage.

Heating was from an open hearth in the centre of the living area. This meant that the main living area had to extend for the full height of the building to allow the smoke to escape through a hole in the roof or a simple form of louvre. If there were any windows they would have had shutters only, as glass was far beyond the means of the occupants of these houses. In the case of the landless labourers, who owned no animals, the house might be of one room only.

A house of this type is clearly alluded to in Chaucer's *Nun's Priest's Tale:* 'Full sooty was her bower and eke her hall.' The 'bower' was an early name for the inner room, and the inner room in this case was apparently open to the roof, any loft over it being open to the hall in the form of a gallery. We are told that the widow who lived here owned 'three large sows', 'three kine', and a sheep as well as Chanticlere the cock and seven hens. These last apparently occupied a perch in the hall itself, but the other animals were probably housed in the byre at the lower end of the house, beyond the entrance doors.

Not surprisingly, no houses of this age and type have survived in their original form, but traces of this type of house, probably dating from the late fifteenth or early sixteenth century, may sometimes be found under later remodelling. This primitive method of building, and the long-house plan, with people and animals under one roof, seems to have survived longer in the north and west of Britain – the highland zone – than it did in the more advanced lowland areas of the south and east. In the Scottish Highlands, houses of this type were in use on the crofts until the eighteenth century.

In these cruck houses, tie-beams were only incorporated in the end walls (where these were not built of solid stone or cob), or where the truss coincided with a partition (fig. 7a). They would have been an obstruction in the main living area or hall. The trusses here were therefore left open and had short 'spurs' – horizontal members attached to them, projecting to the line of the walls, to help support the wall plates (fig. 7b).

An early Welsh long-house reconstructed at the National Museum of Wales, St Fagans.

Thus the cruck truss was a great improvement but with limitations, the main one being that the span and height of the building were limited by the size of the curved timbers available. One solution, common in the West Country, was to construct the cruck from two pieces of timber jointed near the eaves line. This not only enabled shorter timbers to be used, but, as the lower section of the truss or cruck post could be more nearly vertical, it reduced the internal obstruction caused by the older form of cruck (fig 7d).

Box-frame construction

The evolution of the box-frame form of construction followed. In this, the main timber posts, successors to the cruck posts, carried the wall plates, which in turn supported a series of trusses consisting of tie-beams and principal rafters. These trusses carried the ridge piece, and other longitudinal timbers known as purlins, which in turn supported the common rafters (fig. 8a).

A form of roof common in the North at this time had a vertical member, known as a king-post, rising from the tie-beam to support the ridge piece. In districts where stone or cob was used for the walls, rather than timber-framing, this system could be adapted, with the wall plate and the roof structure carried directly on the walls.

45

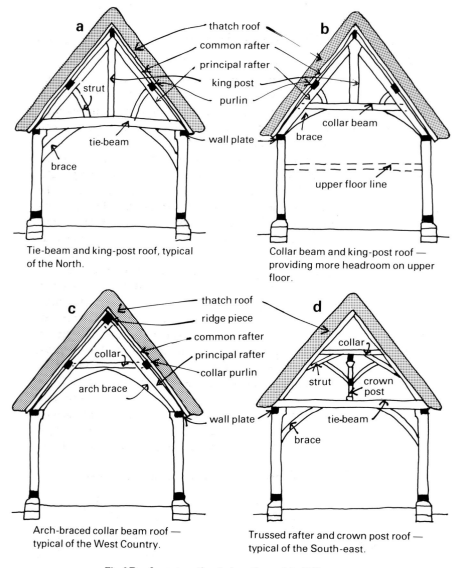

a

thatch roof
common rafter
principal rafter
king post
strut
purlin
tie-beam
wall plate
brace

Tie-beam and king-post roof, typical of the North.

b

collar beam
brace
upper floor line

Collar beam and king-post roof — providing more headroom on upper floor.

c

thatch roof
ridge piece
common rafter
collar
principal rafter
collar purlin
arch brace
wall plate

Arch-braced collar beam roof — typical of the West Country.

d

collar
strut
crown post
tie-beam
brace

Trussed rafter and crown post roof — typical of the South-east.

Fig. 8 **Roof construction in box-framed buildings**

Compared with cruck construction, box-frame construction had several advantages. The building could be higher, allowing for two full storeys where required and more flexibility in the plan. To combat the outward thrust of the roof tie-beams were necessary in every truss, and these could cause an obstruction, visual and actual, in buildings where the walls were still relatively low, as in most small houses with open halls. The logical

46

solution was to replace the tie-beam with a collar beam higher up the roof (fig. 8b). This did not prevent the outward thrust as effectively as a true tie-beam, and various methods were adopted, such as the use of curved braces and wall posts, transferring the weight of the roof lower down the walls. The hammer-beam roof provided the final solution to this problem, as may be seen in many larger halls.

In most of the smaller houses there was less scope for such elaborate roofs. In the West Country the arch-braced collar beam roof was popular (fig. 8c), often strengthened longitudinally by wind-braces which, like other functional features, came to be treated decoratively. In the south-east of Britain, the tie-beam was retained in conjunction with the trussed rafter roof (fig. 8d) which used timbers of smaller section and omitted the larger principal rafters, purlins and wind-bracing. Each pair of rafters was tied by a collar, and these collars were supported at their centres by a longitudinal collar purlin. This collar purlin was supported off the tie-beam by a vertical crown post, from which curved struts radiated to the collars and the collar purlin. The rafters were halved together in pairs at the apex, with no ridge piece. This form of roof is found both in houses and in churches, and it became common in the south-east by the late medieval period. It is found in other areas, but is rare in the south-west of Britain.

In timber-framed buildings of box-frame construction, where there were two or more storeys, the upper storeys were often constructed to overhang the one below, a feature known as 'jettying'. Several reasons have been suggested for this. One was that the overhang, producing a cantilever, reduced the tendency of the upper floors to whip (fig. 9),

Fig. 9 **The cantilever theory of jettied construction (deflection exaggerated)**

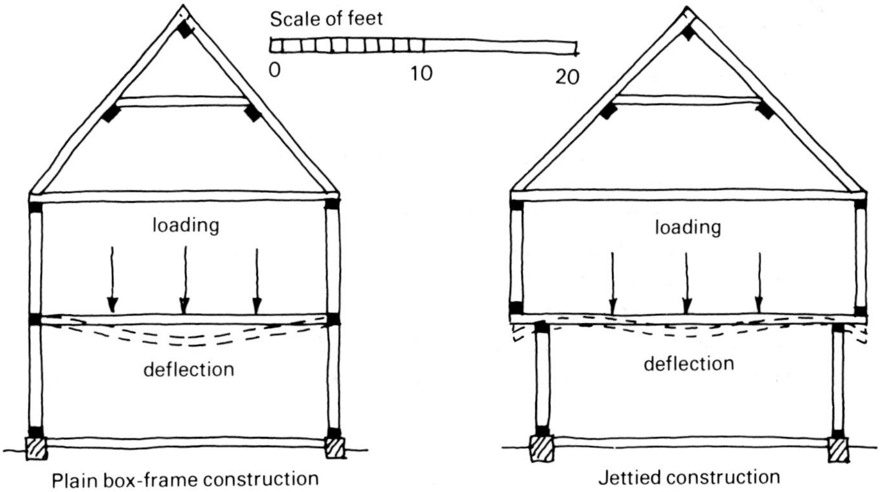

Scale of feet

0   10   20

loading

deflection

Plain box-frame construction

loading

deflection

Jettied construction

Fig. 10 **Typical long-house plan**

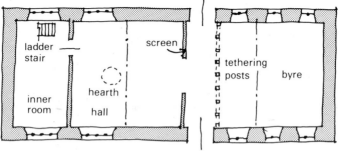

Long-house, typical of the North and West. In this plan, the cross passage, or feeding passage, is generally outside the hall.

particularly since at this period the floor joists were laid flat, not on edge as they are today. Another theory is that the overhanging jetties gave some protection from the weather to the walling below, or simply that they provided more space on the upper floors. On the other hand, the main reason may have been decorative, for the builders of the late Middle Ages took a considerable amount of trouble over the appearance of their work, even in comparatively small houses.

Apart from the change from cruck to box-frame construction, the main improvement in the smaller houses was the removal of the animals to a separate byre or cow house, and the replacement of the byre of the long-house by a service block containing a pantry and buttery. The old through-passage, used for access and for feeding the animals, became a screens passage, so that the plan of the yeoman's house was now a smaller version of that of the manor house.

As with other developments, it appears that this change occurred first in the South-east, probably by the late fourteenth or early fifteenth century. In the North and West, the long-house survived for a century or more after this; indeed some examples still exist where the byre has never been adapted to other uses (fig 10).

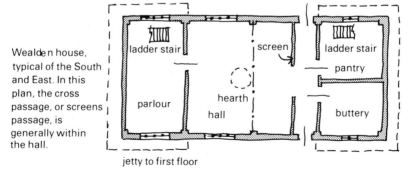

Wealden house, typical of the South and East. In this plan, the cross passage, or screens passage, is generally within the hall.

jetty to first floor

Fig. 11 **Wealden house**

Scale of feet

0   10   20   30

A Wealden house at Hale Street, Kent, probably late fifteenth century. The section to the left of the photograph is a late addition.

The Wealden House

The late medieval and early Tudor yeoman's house, echoing the plan of the manor house, is probably seen at its best in the Weald of Kent and Sussex. This type is often known as the 'Wealden house', although it is found outside this area, with variations. The South-east was an area of great prosperity at this time, when the wool and cloth trades were at their height, and the yeomen farmers, even those with comparatively small holdings, were able to build houses of considerable quality. The plan of these houses is almost standardised, but they vary greatly in size. The interesting fact is that even the smaller examples show a high standard of craftsmanship.

The plan of a typical Wealden house is a simple rectangle, covered by a hipped tiled roof (fig. 11). In the centre is the hall, generally of two bays, with a central crown post and tie-beam truss, and open to the roof. At one end is the parlour (probably used for sleeping), with the solar, also a sleeping room, above it. At the other end, beyond the screens passage and entrance doors, are the pantry and buttery, with either another sleeping room or a store room above them. In the better examples the upper rooms also have crown post trusses.

Cooking was carried out either at the open fire in the hall, or in a

49

The hall of a reconstructed Wealden house at the Weald and Downland Museum, Singleton, Sussex. It illustrates the austere conditions of life even for the more prosperous farmer of the day.

separate kitchen detached from the main house. Access to the upper storeys at each end of the hall was by ladder-type stairs. The hall was lit by a large window at the upper end, some of the larger houses even aspiring to an oriel. The windows were generally unglazed, having square timber mullions (vertical dividing members), set diagonally on plan in a timber head and cill, and fitted with internal sliding shutters. The upper rooms at each end of the house were usually jettied, projecting beyond the walls of the hall. The extra overhanging eaves of the hall in the centre of the house were supported on curved timber brackets.

The Wealden house is found in other parts of Britain, but there are sometimes variations in the design. In some areas, such as East Anglia and Essex, the two-storeyed blocks at each end of the hall are often roofed separately, at right angles to the hall, with projecting gables, and their roofs may be at a higher level than that of the hall.

Sometimes houses are found with a hall and one two-storeyed block or cross-wing only, below the screens passage. In these houses the solar is above the service rooms. These are generally known as 'end hall houses'. The obvious inference is that they were a modification of the Wealden house for a smaller or less prosperous household. This was not always the

A medieval timber-framed house at Lavenham, Suffolk, showing the original open hall between the gabled wings at each end.

51

case, however, for in the Treasurer's House, Martock, Somerset, which is of this form, the fourteenth-century hall was added to an earlier, thirteenth century first-floor hall house, the old first-floor hall becoming the new solar, and the ground floor service room retaining its original function (later converted into a parlour when an external kitchen was added). It may be that the end hall house originated as a modernisation of the first-floor hall house.

As previously mentioned, houses of the Wealden type vary greatly in size. The largest ones differ little if at all from small manor houses, while others would now be described as cottages. Such a description is, however, inaccurate if we accept the definition of a cottage as being the home of a landless labourer or serf – the 'cottar'. Such men, even in late medieval times, could not have afforded even the smallest of the Wealden houses. True cottages at this period were still little more than hovels, and these have not survived.

To summarise, we see that by the end of the Middle Ages there were two main types of farmhouse or yeoman's house being built, the Wealden house and the long-house, having certain features in common: the open hall with its central hearth, with a room partitioned off at one end, probably lofted over and a pair of opposed doors at the other end, generally screened off from the hall. Beyond this area in the Wealden house was a service room, often divided axially into a pantry and a buttery, and short in relation to the length of the hall. The ground floor at the upper end of the hall was probably a sleeping room, or private room for the owner. In the long-house, the room beyond the doors was a byre, or used for some other agricultural or non-domestic purpose, not necessarily screened off completely from the house proper, and often as long as or longer than the hall. It might be open to the roof or lofted over for fodder storage, and its construction was often rougher and poorer than that of the house part. In this type of house the ground floor room at the upper end of the hall was more likely to have been a pantry or other service room.

Some Wealden houses of cruck construction are found away from the South-east, but generally they are of the more advanced box-frame construction. Cruck construction, or one of its adaptations, survived longer in the same areas as did the long-house, and more examples are likely to be found in these areas. In both types of house the first-floor rooms at each end were not always screened off completely from the hall, since signs of smoke-blackening can sometimes be seen on the roof timbers over these rooms, which must therefore have once been galleries open to the hall.

The Treasurer's House, Martock, Somerset. A ground-floor hall added in the late fourteenth century to an earlier first-floor hall house.

A feature found occasionally is an internal jetty over the inner room at the upper end of the hall. In other words, the partition between the hall and the solar, whether it is full height, or simply a gallery front, projects into the hall, above the partition below. It is difficult to see any reason for this feature, except to gain a little more space in the upper room. In larger houses there was sometimes a canopy across the hall at the upper end, over the dais and the high table, and the internal jetty in the smaller houses may be derived from this feature.

Town houses

So far we have looked at houses built in rural areas, occupied by people employed on the land. Town houses possessed many similar features although the long-house is not normally found in towns. The design of the medieval town house was governed largely by lack of space. Land in towns was valuable, and the normal medieval town plot was long and narrow, running back from the street frontage (fig 12).

The usual house plan was rectangular, with a gable end facing on to the street. On the ground floor the front part was often used as a shop or for some other trade purpose. Behind this was the hall, extending through two storeys as in the rural houses. Behind this again was the counting house or office, and perhaps stores and warehouses, with additional living accommodation on upper floors above some or all of these rooms. The kitchen was often a detached structure at the rear, separated from the main house by a courtyard. The upper storey or storeys adjoining the street were usually jettied.

53

Late medieval – probably fifteenth century – town houses in Faversham, Kent, with shops on the ground floor and living accommodation above and at the rear.

The whole house might be raised on a cellar or undercroft, to provide additional storage space or for use as a shop or workshop. Where the frontage was slightly less restricted there might be a front block adjoining the road and parallel to it, linking up with the block at right angles to the road, and forming a T-shaped plan. This enabled a passage to be formed along the side of the rear wing, giving external access to its rooms. Alternatively, on a wider plot, the rear block might be omitted and the block adjoining the road be backed by a parallel block, perhaps containing the living quarters. Where there was adequate land available town houses were planned on similar lines to rural houses, with the main block parallel to the road and either adjoining it or set back behind a forecourt. Sometimes shops would be built along the road frontage enclosing the forecourt, which would be approached from the road through an archway (fig. 13).

As with the rural houses, few medieval town houses have survived in their original form. There has been repeated rebuilding and remodelling of houses on the old sites, and much early construction is now hidden by later work. Many of our old towns are now undergoing large-scale reconstruction, ignoring the old site boundaries. Unless this process is accompanied by careful excavation and recording, much valuable information about early town houses is lost.

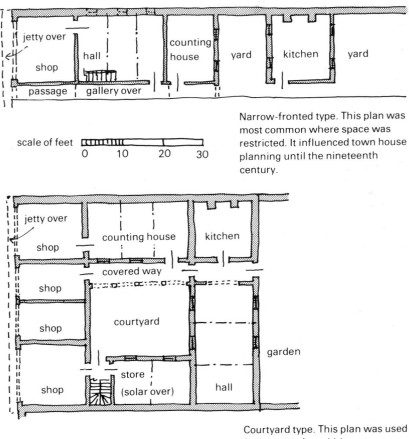

Narrow-fronted type. This plan was most common where space was restricted. It influenced town house planning until the nineteenth century.

Courtyard type. This plan was used for houses of wealthier townspeople where more frontage was available.

Figs. 12 and 13 **Town houses**

55

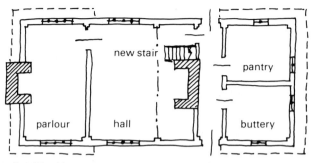

Stack backing on to screens passage

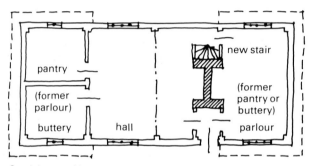

Stack inserted in screens passage

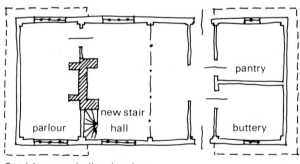

Stack between hall and parlour

All these plans were repeated in
houses first built at this time: two-
storied throughout.

Fig. 14 **Sixteenth and seventeenth century adaptations of medieval farmhouses**

3
Historical development of the house: Tudor revolution

By the end of the fifteenth century there were signs of a major change in the design of the house: the abandonment of the great open hall, a natural consequence of the replacement of the central hearth by a wall fireplace. This change seems first to have occurred in the late medieval priests' houses and other houses connected with the Church, where the rooms on the ground and the first floors appear, from their architectural treatment, to have been of equal importance. In the larger houses the open hall continued in favour throughout the Tudor period, probably for prestige reasons, but it was ceasing to be the main living area of the house, and new houses began to be built with the hall only one storey high.

The changes which began to take place in the design of the larger house reflected a desire for greater comfort and privacy. The breakdown of the communal life of the manor house, leading to a separation of the living quarters of the family from those of the servants, was linked to this. At the same time there was a desire for more ostentation in the design and appearance of the house, perhaps reflecting the rise of a new wealthy class under the Tudors, and the diversion of money and resources from church building to house building, following the Reformation. Under the influence of the Renaissance there was also a desire for more symmetry and formality in the design of the house.

We therefore see the old manor houses being enlarged and modified, and new houses built, reflecting these new influences. We now have to consider how these changes affected the smaller houses, and we find a parallel development occurring but on a simpler scale. As we might expect, the process of altering and rebuilding the older houses began in the more prosperous south-eastern part of Britain, and from there spread gradually north and west.

The period from the mid sixteenth to the later seventeenth century saw a great amount of house building and modernization throughout the whole community, and this must reflect a considerable increase in prosperity and

Continuous jettied houses at Romsey, Hampshire. Traces of the timber-framed construction may be seen under the later plaster on the gable wall.

security. Many houses, large and small, have survived from this period — a tribute to the quality of their construction.

Changes in design

In the medieval period chimneys were rare in the smaller houses, but by the sixteenth century they were becoming more common. The earliest form was the smoke-bay or fire hood, constructed of lath and plaster, within the open hall; but these were later superseded by brick or stone structures. Indeed, in areas lacking good building stone, where most houses were built of timber-framing, it was the introduction of brick in Tudor times that made possible the construction of safe and effective chimneys. This meant that the old open hearth was done away with, and with it went the need for the hall to be open to the roof. Among the smaller houses very few open halls have survived in their original form.

There is evidence in some houses, however, that the insertion of the chimney was not followed immediately by the flooring over of the hall. This may be paralleled in the larger houses, where many open halls survive, with wall fireplaces. It seems that the insertion of the chimney was the first 'improvement' to be carried out, perhaps in emulation of the

58

larger houses. It was then realised that the hall need no longer be open to the roof, and that an inserted floor would not only facilitate heating, but would provide an additional room without having to enlarge the house. The open halls must have been cold and draughty, and their soot-blackened roof timbers show the inefficiency of the smoke louvres or vents.

At this period, also, window glass was becoming cheaper, so that windows were usually glazed instead of being shuttered. Larger windows, with leaded glazing and iron opening lights, were often inserted into older houses.

New houses were now built two-storeyed throughout, and in the areas where timber-framing was the usual method of construction, they often had continuous jetties.

Conversions of older houses

The conversion of the Wealden houses could be carried out in a number of ways. Sometimes the new chimney stack was inserted in the hall, backing on to the screens passage and converting it into a solid through-passage. This had the effect of reducing the size of the hall, particularly since the early chimney stacks were very massive. A spiral or newel stair was generally inserted adjoining this stack, replacing the old ladders leading from the open hall to the upper rooms at each end. Sometimes a second chimney stack was built to serve the parlour, generally on the end wall. The hall now became in effect the farmhouse kitchen, with the pantry and buttery beyond the passage remaining in use as before (fig. 14a).

Another method of conversion, particularly popular where the original hall was already small, was to insert the stack in the screens passage, doing away with the passage itself, and leaving only a lobby inside the front door. This meant that the stack could have two fireplaces on the ground floor. In this scheme the old pantry and buttery were sometimes converted into a heated parlour, the old parlour becoming a pantry. Again, a newel staircase was fitted in behind the chimney stack, blocking the old back door (fig. 14b).

A third alternative was to insert the stack between the hall and the parlour, leaving the screens passage and service rooms intact (fig. 14c).

When an end hall house was converted, the stack might be inserted backing on to the screens passage, or it might be built on the end wall of the hall, leaving the screens passage unaltered.

When the hall was floored over as part of the conversion scheme, the central tie-beam of the roof was left in an inconvenient position a few feet above the new first-floor level. It was therefore sometimes removed, and the roof remodelled at the same time. Dormer windows might be inserted also to light the new upper room. For structural reasons, it was not always possible to insert the new floor over the hall at the same level as those floors already existing at each end of the house. Unexplained changes in the first-floor levels in an old house sometimes provide a clue that it originally had an open hall.

In many of the surviving long-houses, generally of cruck or cruck-type construction, a similar conversion was carried out. The byre was rebuilt or converted to form a kitchen, often with an added chimney stack on the end gable wall. In a cruck-framed house, the removal of the tie-beam above the new first floor caused fewer problems than it did in a box-frame building, since it was not strictly a tie, and was not needed to prevent the roof from spreading. Its removal simply meant that the wall plate had to be supported in some other way, usually by the wall itself.

Since the byre was often of poorer construction than the main part of the house, rebuilding rather than conversion was often necessary. Evidence that the kitchen and service rooms beyond a through-passage have been rebuilt may suggest that a house was originally a long-house. The size of the lower end is also significant in this context. The pantry and buttery block of a Wealden house was normally quite short compared to the size of the hall, whereas the byre of a long-house was often almost as long as the hall. Another difference between the two basic house types may be seen in the position of the through-passage. In the Wealden house, this is usually within the hall, that is, the end truss of the hall is above the partition between the through-passage and the service rooms. In the long-house the passage is usually outside the hall, with the end truss of the hall above the partition between the hall and the through-passage. The passage in this type of house was in effect part of the byre. These differences are particularly interesting in areas at the junction of the highland and lowland zones, where both Wealden and long-houses are found.

At this period of increasing prosperity, the older houses were not only modernized internally, but were often enlarged. Owing to the limitations of the roof construction, and the fact that most traditional roofing materials required a steep pitch, houses were still normally only one room deep, with perhaps a single-storey lean-to addition at the rear over which the main roof slope could be continued. Houses were normally enlarged either by lengthening them by one or more rooms, or by adding wings to form a T or L-shaped plan. Sometimes the new addition took the form of a kitchen and service wing, perhaps replacing an old detached kitchen, or even

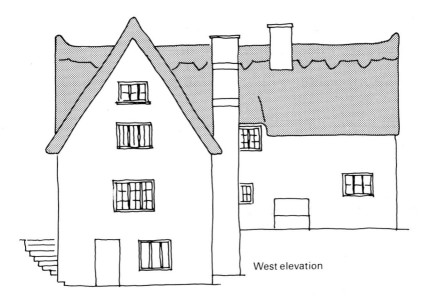

West elevation

Fig 15. and fig. 16 (overleaf) **The Potash, Cretingham, Suffolk. A farmhouse,** of late sixteenth or early seventeenth century date; timber-framed and plastered, with a thatch roof – now of Norfolk Reed. The plan is derived from that of the medieval Wealden type house with a chimney stack between the hall and the parlour. It is not clear whether the parlour was originally heated. In the later seventeenth century the house was enlarged by building a new parlour wing, taking advantage of the fall of the ground to provide a cellar and an attic. The original parlour was probably converted to a kitchen at this time. The newel stair in the later wing is original, but the stair in the older block was inserted when the house was divided into two cottages and has since been removed. The site of the original stair in this wing is not known. The timber-framed walls of this house were probably always plastered. The roof shows the up-swept gables typical of East Anglian thatch.

East elevation

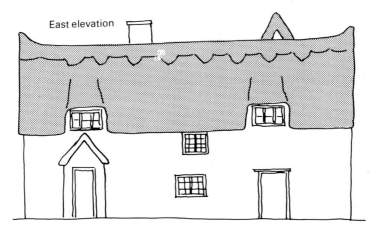

The Potash, Cretingham, Suffolk. An attic storey was incorporated in the higher wing added at the rear.

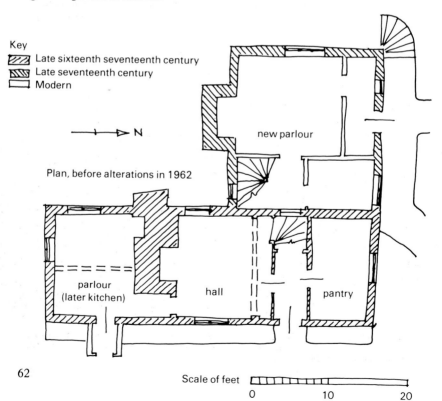

Key
Late sixteenth seventeenth century
Late seventeenth century
Modern

N

Plan, before alterations in 1962

new parlour

parlour
(later kitchen)

hall

pantry

Scale of feet

0   10   20

incorporating such a structure into the house. In other cases the new wing consisted of a parlour, sometimes on a rather grander scale than that of the original house.

New houses

The alternative ways of modernizing the late medieval and early Tudor farmhouses were reflected in the plans of new houses being built from the mid sixteenth to the mid seventeenth century. Indeed, at first sight it is often difficult to tell whether a late Tudor or Stuart house was built in its present form, or whether it is a remodelling of an earlier house. A rebuilt lower end will provide a clue, but often a detailed inspection will be necessary to decide whether the first floor over the hall, and the chimney stacks, are integral with the main structure or later insertions. If evidence of smoke-blackening is found on the roof timbers, the early origin of the house is confirmed.

As we have seen, the most usual development from the long-house was the removal of the animals to a separate building, and the replacement of the byre by a kitchen. In some areas, however, a different development

House at Hazelbury Bryan, Dorset. A three-room house with a central stack and lobby entrance, probably seventeenth century, derived from the plan shown in fig. 14 (centre).

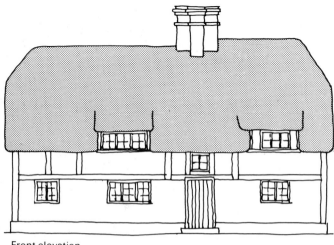

Front elevation

Fig. 17 **Saint John's, Hinton Martel, Dorset. An early seventeenth century
farmhouse, built two-storeyed throughout, but echoing the plan of the typical
medieval house with the stack inserted in the cross passage, creating a lobby
entrance. The parlour is as large as the hall, indicating its increasing importance
at this period. The house was originally timber-framed, but much of the ground
storey has been rebuilt in brick.**

The first-floor rooms were originally open to the roof, and may have been used
as stores or workrooms rather than bedrooms. In the later seventeenth century
these rooms were ceiled, and the dormer windows inserted, probably indicating a
change in the status of the rooms. The dormers were originally of oriel form, and
traces of their moulded oak heads may be seen above the more modern casements. The stair in the pantry was probably inserted when the house was divided
into two cottages.

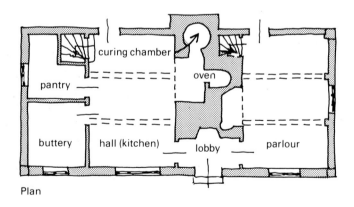

Plan

Scale of feet

0   10   20

St Johns, Hinton Martel. The projecting moulded head of a former oriel window can be seen above a more recent casement.

took place. Here the byre, perhaps combined with a barn, remained attached to the house, but there was no longer any internal connection between them (fig. 18). This type of house is called a Laithe house, and it is most common in Yorkshire, where houses of this type were built from the seventeenth to the nineteenth centuries. The house part is generally small in relation to the Laithe or farm building. Laithe houses seem to have been built as a rule by small farmers, and on marginal or newly cultivated

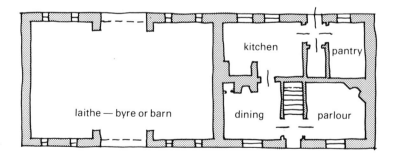

Fig. 18 **Typical Laithe house plan. The house plans vary considerably, and in later examples may be of double-pile form. The 'Laithe' may comprise a barn, or a byre, with a hay loft above it.**

65

A simple two-roomed house at Corfe Castle, Dorset, with an end chimney stack. See the plan shown in fig. 19b.

land. Although they are found in several parts of the country as well as in Yorkshire, they are less common in the more prosperous farming areas, and are probably the product of a more primitive form of agriculture.

Smaller farmhouses

Apart from the plans directly derived from those of late medieval houses, other types are found in houses of the late sixteenth and seventeenth centuries, with two main rooms only on each floor. The insertion of the chimney stack in the screens passage produced the 'lobby entrance' plan with three rooms, two on one side of the stack and one on the other. A similar plan, but with two rooms only was clearly derived from this (fig. 19a), and an even simpler plan was that having two rooms, one heated by a chimney stack on the end gable wall, and the other unheated (fig. 19b). This plan may have been derived from the typical medieval plan, omitting the through-passage and lower room. In some cases, particularly early in the period, the entrance is found in the end gable wall next to the chimney stack, which supports this theory. In later examples, it is more usual to find the entrance in the front wall, leading either into the 'hall' or heated room, or into the unheated room.

Although these two-roomed houses were presumably built by less wealthy occupants than the three-roomed houses, they were still probably

Fig. 19 Smaller farmhouses of the seventeenth to eighteenth centuries

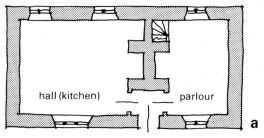

hall (kitchen)   parlour

a

Two-room lobby entrance plan
A smaller version of the type derived from the insertion of the stack in the cross-passage

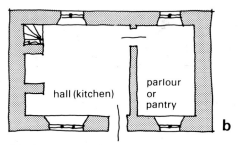

hall (kitchen)   parlour or pantry

b

Simple two-room plan

This type, with a heated hall and an unheated inner room would have been built by the smaller farmers. In its humblest form it might be of one storey only.

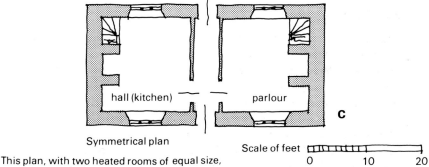

hall (kitchen)   parlour

c

Symmetrical plan

Scale of feet

0   10   20

This plan, with two heated rooms of equal size, shows the growing influence of the Renaissance.

the homes of yeomen or husbandmen, and not the 'cottages' of the landless labourers. These latter were still often of one room and one storey only. Although few of them have survived, large numbers were being built at this time. The prevailing change from arable to sheep farming in Britain, while bringing prosperity for some, meant unemployment and destitution for many others, and this was creating a social problem. In 1588 an Act of Parliament was passed to try to control the building of cottages. It stated that no cottage was to be built unless it had at least four acres of land with it, either adjoining the cottage, or in the open fields. The purpose of the Act was clearly to prevent the growth of rural slums, but like much other building legislation of the time it was largely ignored.

In the case of houses with a three-room plan as previously described, the type with a chimney stack backing on to the through-passage was more common in the West Country, while the lobby entrance plan with the stack inserted in the screens passage predominated in the South-east at this time. The lobby entrance plan provided the parlour with its own entrance; it did not have to be entered through the hall. This may indicate that the parlour was becoming a more important room, perhaps a private living room rather than a sleeping room, and it could explain the earlier popularity of this plan in the more advanced parts of the country. In a few cases, in houses with the stack backing on to the passage, the room below the passage was a parlour, not the more usual kitchen or pantry. This indicates the same development of the parlour as an increasingly important room in relation to the hall.

From the late sixteenth to the early eighteenth century we sometimes find two farmhouses built close together, even attached, apparently sharing the farm buildings and land. Documentary evidence may indicate that they were built for different members, or different generations, of the same family still farming the land as one unit, and they are known as 'Unit houses'. When the two houses are detached, their origin is relatively easy to identify, but sometimes two attached houses have been made into one at a later date by forming openings through the original party walls. The plan of the resulting house may be difficult to interpret until this possibility is appreciated. These houses often appear to be deliberately planned to avoid one house overlooking the other. The two units may have been built together, or differ in date, perhaps only by one generation, say forty or fifty years.

Architectural changes

With the disappearance of the open hall came a change in roof design. Since the roof was no longer visible, the more decorative forms passed out of use. In the south-east of England, crown post roofs ceased to be constructed after the end of the sixteenth century, as did the ornamental

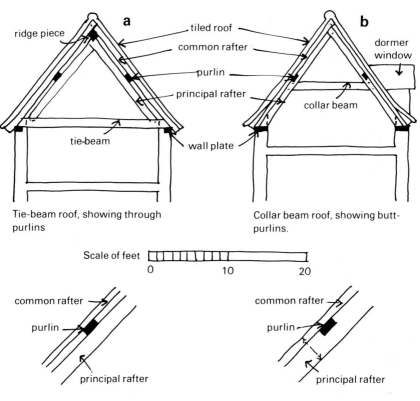

a

ridge piece

tiled roof

common rafter

purlin

principal rafter

tie-beam

wall plate

b

dormer window

collar beam

Tie-beam roof, showing through purlins

Collar beam roof, showing butt-purlins.

Scale of feet

0   10   20

common rafter

purlin

principal rafter

common rafter

purlin

principal rafter

Through-purlin type, commonest in North and West, succeeding cruck and king-post construction.

Butt-purlin type, commonest in South and East, succeeding trussed rafter and crown post construction.

Fig. 20 **Roof construction in smaller houses – late sixteenth to early eighteenth centuries.**

arch-braced collar beam roofs in the West Country. In some areas, cruck and jointed cruck roofs continued in use into the seventeenth century, but by the end of the century the normal roof consisted of common rafters supported on purlins, spanning between plain tie-beam trusses (fig. 20a). In the smaller houses, where the first-floor rooms were partly in the roof, the tie-beam was often replaced by a collar beam (fig. 20b).

Although at this period there were considerable changes in the planning of the house, and an increase in its comfort and privacy, there was less change in architectural style. So far, most of the smaller and medium sized houses, particularly in rural areas, were affected little if at all by the influence of the Renaissance. Architectural detail was essentially late medieval. Roofs were steeply pitched and generally gabled, except where the influence of the true Wealden house predominated. Windows had

69

An early Tudor shop at Cerne Abbas, Dorset. The large windows would originally have been fitted with shutters.

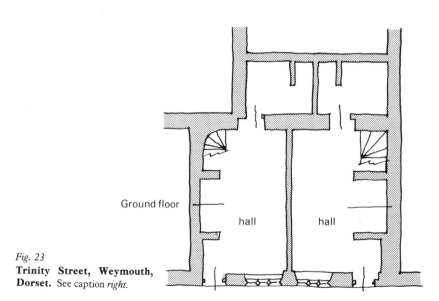

Ground floor

hall hall

Fig. 23
Trinity Street, Weymouth, Dorset. See caption *right.*

70

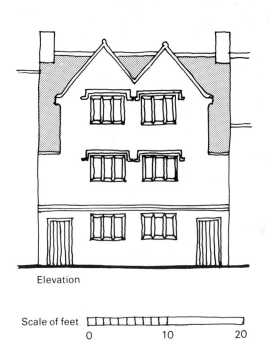

Elevation

Scale of feet

0   10   20

Fig. 22 and fig. 23 (below) **Trinity Street, Weymouth, Dorset. This pair of small town houses, near the waterfront, probably dates from the late sixteenth century. They each consist of one room only on each floor, and their small size contrasts with the high quality of craftsmanship in their construction. The facade is of finely cut Portland Stone ashlar, and their builders must have been relatively wealthy. The ground-floor room in each house always appears to have been heated, and was presumably the hall, or main living room, with sleeping rooms on the two upper floors. If there was a kitchen it was probably a separate structure at the rear, now vanished.**

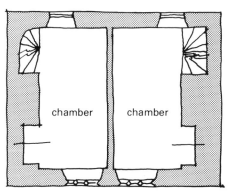

First floor

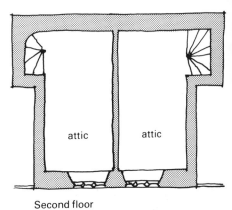

Second floor

71

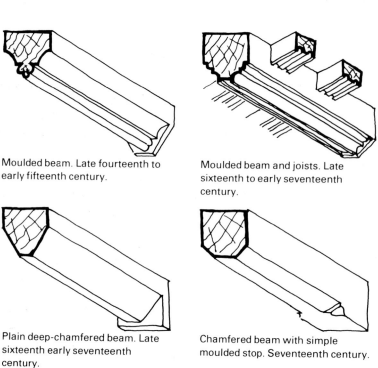

Moulded beam. Late fourteenth to early fifteenth century.

Moulded beam and joists. Late sixteenth to early seventeenth century.

Plain deep-chamfered beam. Late sixteenth early seventeenth century.

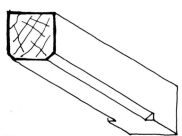

Chamfered beam with simple moulded stop. Seventeenth century.

Hollow-chamfered beam with pyramid stop. Seventeenth century.

Plain stop-chamfered beam. Found in simple buildings until the early eighteenth century. The small chamfers indicate later date.

Fig. 21 **Ceiling beams – details. Dates are approximate only, as there are considerable regional variations. Beams with differing detail in a building generally indicate different building dates.**

moulded mullions of stone or timber, with leaded lights in iron opening casements. Doors often retained a four-centred arched head. The separate hood-moulds above door and window openings only began to be replaced by continuous string courses by the late seventeenth century, when a few tentative classical details appeared, generally around the main entrance door, on houses of the wealthier farmers who had come into contact with the latest architectural fashions. Internally, the timber beams and joists supporting the upper floors were still exposed. In the more important rooms these beams might be moulded, or have their angles splayed off or chamfered, these chamfers being stopped at their ends in a variety of patterns (fig. 21).

Only at the end of this period, after the Restoration of King Charles II, do we find the desire for more formal design, in particular for a symmetrical elevation, beginning to affect the smaller and medium sized houses. Until now, the elevation of the house had simply reflected the plan, but by the late seventeenth century the plan was being adapted to fit behind a symmetrically designed elevation. This was not achieved immediately. Many houses can be found with an almost symmetrical facade, showing that function had not yet been entirely subordinated to fashion.

In its simplest form, the symmetrical plan consisted of two rooms separated by a central through-passage, each room having a chimney stack in its end gable wall. This plan may be derived from the three-room plan with a through-passage, omitting the inner room or parlour at the end of the hall.

Town houses

In the towns, as in the rural areas, much rebuilding and modernization of older houses took place at this time. Due to the restricted sites of many town houses, there was often little scope for actual expansion. Houses might be extended at the rear over the old narrow gardens and yards, and there was a certain amount of 'backland' development: putting up blocks of small houses and cottages at the back of the narrow plots.

Houses were also increased in height, and jettying here had the advantage of providing increased accommodation on the upper floors. The front part of the ground floor of the typical town house was still often used as a shop, and the actual shop fronts at this period differed little from those of the Middle Ages. They were normally unglazed and fitted with wooden shutters, which were hinged to open and form a counter during the day, and secured shut at night.

In town houses, as elsewhere, the old open halls were floored over and chimney stacks inserted. New houses were built two-storeyed throughout from the start. Timber-framing was still much used for town houses, although the dividing walls between houses were sometimes of stone or brick, presumably to reduce the risk of fire spreading from one building to

Seventeenth century houses in Portsmouth, Hampshire. The Flemish style gables were popular at this period. Sash windows were inserted in the eighteenth century.

another. Brick was also becoming more common for complete buildings, particularly in towns.

The shortage of building land in towns also led to encroachment on the streets themselves. Contrary to popular belief, the main streets of many medieval towns were quite wide, opening out into a large market area in the centre of the town. The market was occupied by stalls, and there was a tendency for these to become permanent. Eventually they might be replaced by permanent shops, with living accommodation above them. Often in an old town we may come across a triangular or rectangular block of buildings, surrounded by narrow streets. On investigation this may prove to be an encroachment on the original market area.

In the towns, the houses of the wealthy merchants were often elaborately and quite ostentatiously designed, and here the influence of the Renaissance was generally seen earlier than it was in rural areas. A Flemish

Contrasting materials in early seventeenth century town merchants' houses. Stone at Hexham, Northumberland, shown here, and timber-framing at Frankwell, Shrewsbury, below.

Elevation

Fig. 24 **Churche's Mansion, Nantwich, Cheshire. Elevation and ground floor plan.**

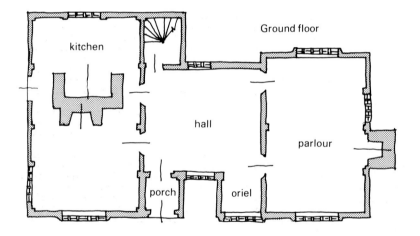

Ground floor

kitchen

hall

parlour

porch

oriel

character is often discernible in the design, a reminder of the prosperous trade with the Low Countries at this time.

At the other end of the social scale, blocks and terraces of very small cottages were being built for urban artisans, apparently as a speculation, and let out for rent. This development had begun in medieval times, and increased with the need to accommodate a growing urban population. It was to have a lasting effect on the character of English towns.

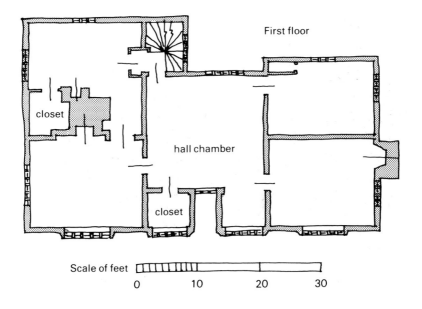

First floor

closet

hall chamber

closet

Scale of feet

0   10   20   30

Fig. 25 **Churche's Mansion, Nantwich, Cheshire. In towns, where sufficient land was available, houses were planned on similar lines to those in rural areas. Richard Churche, a wealthy merchant and landowner, had this house built in 1577, a fact recorded in an inscription cut on the front of the house. The design of the house shows the typical Elizabethan adaptation of the medieval plan. The hall is single-storeyed, with a chamber above it. There is no screens passage, the site of the rear doorway being occupied by a staircase block. The hall is not heated, suggesting that it was used as a circulation area rather than a living room. The parlour is larger than the hall. At the lower end, in the service block, the rear room appears to have been the kitchen. The front room may have been a buttery, but, being heated, it was perhaps used as an office or counting-house. The house is of timber-framed construction, showing the ornamental framing typical of the North-west.**

Apart from this house and its outbuildings, which included dovecotes and stables, Richard Churche owned a considerable amount of land and other property, both in Nantwich itself and as far away as Stafford. The house is thus of interest as a dated example of the home of a wealthy merchant at a time of increasing prosperity for this class. In succeeding centuries, many houses of this type have been refaced externally and divided into tenements, hiding their original form, and in many cases leading to their demolition, in ignorance of their true character.

4

Historical development of the house: the last three hundred years

By the late seventeenth century the influence of the Renaissance was seen not only in the larger houses but in those of medium size, and it was soon to affect the design of even the smallest houses.

In the larger country houses the rather rambling medieval plan, with its central hall and flanking wings, generally one room deep, was giving way to a compact rectangular plan, designed behind a symmetrical facade. The influence of the medieval tower house can be seen in the Lodge houses popular in the early seventeenth century. These were rectangular or square in plan, originally designed for occasional rather than permanent occupation, and were evolved from the medieval hunting lodges.

The change of plan which was to affect houses of all classes was soon accompanied by changes in architectural style, in particular the replacement of traditional Gothic features by the newly fashionable Classical details. Four-centred Tudor arches were replaced by classical hoods and pediments. Mullioned and transomed casement windows were giving way to double-hung sashes. Gables were replaced by hipped roofs, and eventually in all prestigious houses the main roofs were largely hidden behind parapets.

The hall, from being the main living area, had become simply an entrance and central circulation area, albeit a very grand one in some cases. While the open hall had predominated, staircases were given little architectural prominence, but by the late seventeenth century the staircase was beginning to become an important feature, and by the eighteenth century was often the principal feature of the entrance hall.

The use of brick was becoming more popular, replacing timber-framing in areas where good stone was not available.

Single-fronted Georgian terrace houses at Worcester. A good example of eighteenth century urban layout.

Windsbatch Farm House, Upwey, Dorset. A symmetrical house of the seventeenth century. The architectural details are still Gothic in character.

Farmhouses

In the smaller houses, particularly in rural areas, classical features were slower to appear, and in some remote areas such details as mullioned windows and gables continued to be built into the eighteenth century. Even at this social level, however, a symmetrical plan was thought desirable, and the typical small farmhouse of the late seventeenth and early eighteenth centuries had a central door leading into a through-passage, with the main rooms of equal size on either side of this, and chimneys in the end gable walls (fig. 26). The service rooms were generally at the back in a single-storey lean-to, but they were sometimes fitted into the main block between the through-passage and the main rooms. There were generally spiral staircases adjoining the chimney stacks at each end of the house, avoiding the need for inter-communicating rooms on the first floor. At a later date these rather cramped spiral stairs were sometimes replaced by a new straight-flight stair inserted in the through-passage.

There were some variations on this plan: sometimes the front door led not into a through-passage but into a lobby with an unheated service room behind it, part of which was cut off to provide space for a staircase.

The one-room-deep, or single-pile plan, with a single-storey lean-to at the rear, was eventually superseded by the double-pile plan, two rooms deep and two-storeyed throughout, with the chimney stacks either in the

80

end gable walls as before or sited inside the house on the central spine wall. This plan enabled the kitchen and service rooms to be fitted neatly behind the main rooms, hidden from public view. The adoption of this plan caused some problems of roof construction, since most traditional roofing materials required a steep roof pitch. To start with the roof was often constructed in two parallel ranges, with a central valley gutter. This could cause maintenance problems, and sometimes the central area between the

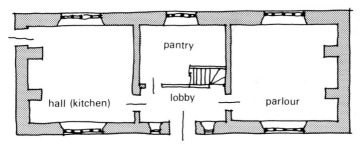

Three-roomed symmetrical plan (one
unheated service room)

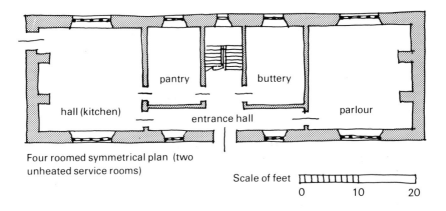

Four roomed symmetrical plan (two
unheated service rooms)

Scale of feet
0   10   20

Fig. 26 **Larger farmhouses of the seventeenth to eighteenth centuries. By the late seventeenth century the influence of the Renaissance had reached most parts of the country. A symmetrical facade was now considered essential, and various means were used to fit the necessary farmhouse accommodation behind this. The hall had now become in effect the kitchen, and was the same size as the parlour. The cross passage was often abandoned, access to the farmyard being direct from the kitchen.**

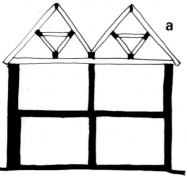
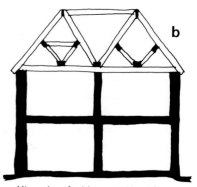

Double-pitch roof with central valley gutter. Probably the earliest double-pile roof form. The central valley could cause problems of maintenance.

Hipped roof with central lead flat. Overcame the problem of the central valley with the same general appearance.

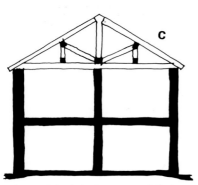
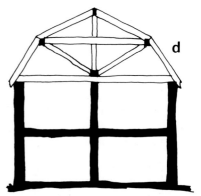

Low-pitched single-span roof. Only practicable with slates or pantiles. Became common in all areas when improved transport made these materials generally available.

Mansard roof. Provided attic space; became common when slate was available for the flatter upper slope.

Scale of feet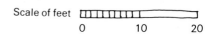

0   10   20

Fig. 27 **Roofing the double-pile house**

ridges was covered with a flat lead roof. Later, after improved transport made Welsh slates available over most of England, roofs could be constructed at a lower pitch, and a double-pile house could be roofed in one span. Sometimes a mansard roof was preferred, providing useful attic space (fig. 27).

Historical development: The last three hundred years

By the middle of the eighteenth century classical details had taken over even in the smaller houses, and this country Georgian style is often very attractive. The eighteenth century was a time of considerable change in farming practice, and in many areas this meant increased prosperity. This found expression both in the building of new farmhouses, and the alteration of older ones. In areas where farming had been carried out on the open field system, the farmhouses and other buildings were sited in the village street itself. Following the Parliamentary Enclosures in the

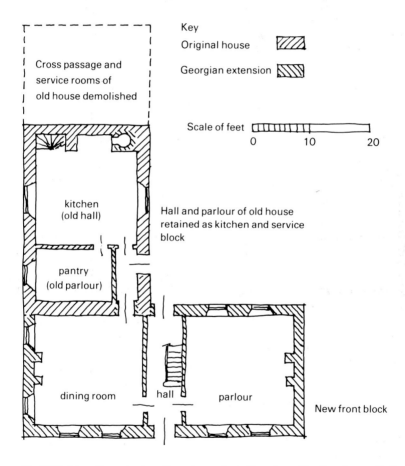

Fig. 28 **Eighteenth or nineteenth century adaptation of an older farmhouse. In the eighteenth and early nineteenth centuries many older farmhouses were rebuilt. Sometimes, however, part of the old house was retained as the kitchen block, behind the new, classical styled house.**

century, these old farms were sometimes provided with complete new farmhouses and sets of farm buildings in the centre of the newly enclosed fields. Often the old farmhouses were divided at this time into cottages for the farmworkers, some of whom were the former small farmers who had lost their land following the Enclosures. In other cases, the old farmhouses were retained and modernized, or rebuilt on their old sites.

This rebuilding or modernization of farmhouses also occurred on farms which had always been in isolated situations: early enclosures, representing clearance of the forest or heath by individual family groups, for the open field system had not been universal even in medieval times. A farmhouse might not always be completely rebuilt. The old house, or the best part of it, was sometimes retained as the kitchen wing, while a new Georgian block was added at the front, containing the best rooms (fig. 28).

Town houses

In the towns, where sufficient space was available, many medium sized Georgian houses were built, of the same basic form as the farmhouses previously described. The most usual plan was two rooms deep, two or three storeys high, perhaps with an attic, and a cellar or basement. In these town houses one or both of the front rooms on the ground floor might be used for business purposes, with the living rooms facing the garden at the rear, and the kitchen and service rooms in the basement. Both in town and country houses the main front elevation generally had a range of five windows on each of the upper floors and four on the ground floor, with a central doorway. Brick was now the most usual material, although stone was used in areas where it was available. Occasionally, timber-framing was still used, but this was now almost always covered with plaster, tile-hanging, weatherboarding, or 'mathematical' tiles — designed to imitate brickwork.

The windows were usually double-hung sashes, and the main entrance door was given emphasis by a hood or pediment, sometimes flanked by pilasters, or a projecting columned porch.

Although this type of house was almost standardized in plan and general design there were many variations in detail. Most houses of this type and period are very attractive, and find a ready market today.

Not all Georgian houses were of this double-fronted plan. In the older towns the medieval layout, with its long narrow plots, still governed house design, and it was probably the rebuilding of houses on these sites that

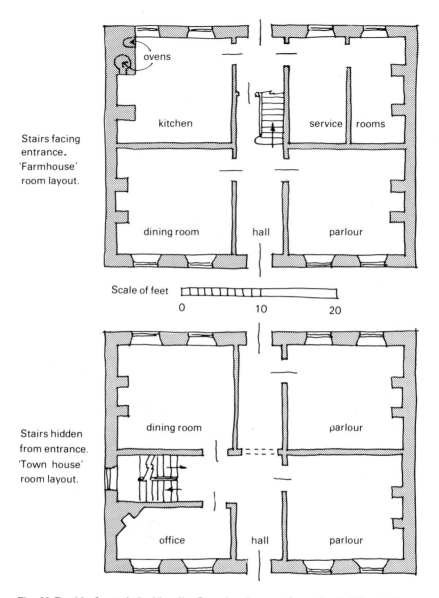

Stairs facing
entrance.
'Farmhouse'
room layout.

ovens

kitchen

service | rooms

dining room | hall | parlour

Scale of feet

0   10   20

Stairs hidden
from entrance.
'Town house'
room layout.

dining room

parlour

office | hall | parlour

Fig. 29 **Double-fronted double-pile Georgian houses.** Once the builders had overcome the problem of roofing the double-pile house, house plans became more compact. Georgian double-fronted town houses were similar to the farmhouses of the period, differing only in the uses to which the ground-floor rooms were put. In the farmhouse, the dining room and parlour were generally at the front, with the kitchen and service rooms at the rear. In a town house, one or both of the front rooms might be used for trade or business purposes, with living rooms at the rear, overlooking the garden. Sometimes the main living room-the withdrawing room-was on the first floor. The kitchen and service rooms were often in a basement, making more use of a restricted town site.

A double-fronted eighteenth century town house at Ottery St Mary, Devon.

produced the plan of the typical Georgian terrace house (fig. 30). In this the door led into an entrance hall containing the staircase, with rooms on one side of this only. In its simplest form the house was two rooms deep, but there might be smaller additional rooms at the rear. Even when the ground floor was not used for business purposes, the principal living rooms were often on the first-floor. There was sometimes a basement, containing the kitchen and service rooms.

Shop fronts were glazed and divided into small panes, the window generally being given a classical frame with a cornice and pilasters of painted timber. Bow windows were popular for shops, but were not universal. Their widespread revival today has given some eighteenth century streets rather a bogus period character. The effect is particularly unfortunate when manufacturers' ready-made standard windows are introduced, unrelated to the design of the building or to genuine eighteenth century examples.

A house in Cathedral Close, Exeter, probably an eighteenth century remodelling of an earlier building, as the character of the stonework shows.

An eighteenth century shop front at Beaminster, Dorset. The owner's house, to the left of the photograph, formed one building with the shop.

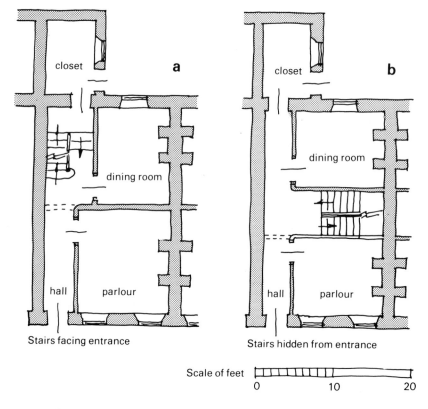

Fig. 30 **Single-fronted town houses – eighteenth and nineteenth centuries.**

In many cases in old towns, a house was not completely rebuilt in the eighteenth century, but was simply given a face-lift, and a Georgian facade often hides a much earlier building.

Building in many towns was not confined to rebuilding on old individual sites. The population of the country was expanding, and some towns were growing fast. Speculative development of whole areas was beginning to have a great impact on the town scene. A builder would buy or lease an area of land, often on the outskirts of a town no longer confined by its medieval walls, and would lay out terraces and squares. He might let the plots on lease for others to develop, or build the houses himself for subsequent sale or letting. Generally the original developer exercised control over the design of the houses, at least as far as their main elevations were concerned. Thus we see whole areas developed in accordance with a unified design. Bath provides some particularly good examples of this.

The individual houses created in this way were generally of the single-

Part of The Circus, Bath. The whole city is a notable example of comprehensive town development in the eighteenth century.

fronted plan derived from the medieval street layout, and this remained the typical town house design until well into the nineteenth century.

The early developers in this field were mainly private entrepreneurs such as Nicholas Barbon, who was active in London after the Great Fire of 1666. Later, in the eighteenth century, the large landed estates began to see the profits which could be made from large-scale developments, particularly in the growing areas of west London. Much of the development carried out by the Portman, Bedford, Grosvenor and other large estates survives today. Some of this was on quite a grand scale. The streets were wide, and the buildings were spaced sufficiently far apart to allow not only for good rear gardens, but for coach houses and stables to be built in mews courts between the terraces of houses.

These simple early nineteenth century artisans' cottages in Shrewsbury are given some distinction by their iron balconies, and the door hoods show the influence of the Greek Revival. Their well-cared-for appearance indicates their changed social status today.

From the early eighteenth century, building in English towns was to be controlled increasingly by Acts of Parliament, and by local regulations and bye-laws. Some attempt at this control had been made earlier, in Elizabethan and Jacobean times, mainly in an attempt to prevent over-crowding and the spread of fire, but these early regulations had often been ignored. By the eighteenth century, however, stricter controls were introduced, and these were to influence house design, particularly the main facade. One important effect of the regulations was a reduction in the amount of timber exposed on the facade, and this resulted, indirectly, in an increasing standardization of design, particularly in such details as doorways and windows.

Another influence with a similar effect was the appearance of a large number of architectural pattern books, providing drawings of suitable details for different categories of houses. Other legal measures which affected the design and appearance of houses, in rural areas as well as in the towns, were the Window Tax which was introduced in 1695 and lasted through the eighteenth century, and a tax on bricks introduced in 1784 and removed in 1850. The tax on bricks encouraged the use of other materials,

Early nineteenth century terrace houses in Shrewsbury, showing the influence of the Greek Revival.

Early nineteenth century houses at Clerkenwell, London, of a humbler type than the examples shown at Exeter and Shrewsbury. The minimal exposed timber on the facade shows the effects of the London Building Acts.

Southernhay, Exeter. Early nineteenth century town houses continuing the Georgian tradition. The doorway details are in Coade stone.

and may have contributed to the increasing popularity of external plaster or stucco in the late eighteenth and early nineteenth centuries.

Old timber-framed houses were often refaced during this period, partly for reasons of fashion, and partly to improve their weather resistance. Sometimes a timber-framed building was completely faced, or had its outer walls rebuilt, in brick. Sometimes the timbers were simply covered with plaster, tile-hanging, or weather boarding. Mathematical tiles were also popular, as they gave the effect of brickwork, but were not taxed.

A face-lift of this kind was often accompanied by the insertion of new sash windows in place of the old casements, and the roof might be remodelled to provide additional headroom in the upper storey.

Cottages

We have seen how the agricultural developments of the eighteenth century resulted in the building of new farmhouses and the improvement of older ones, all indicative of increased prosperity for the larger farmers, who profited from the Enclosures. This prosperity was not always shared by the

Fig. 31 **Blaise Hamlet, Henbury, Bristol. Blaise Hamlet was built in about 1811 by John Harford, the owner of Blaise Castle Estate, as a 'model' village for the estate pensioners. It was designed by John Nash, assisted by G. S. Repton, and is one of the best surviving examples of the Picturesque Movement.**

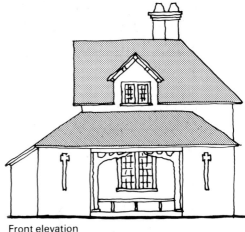

Front elevation

Scale of feet

0   10

Cottage no. 7 — from G. S. Repton's sketchbook

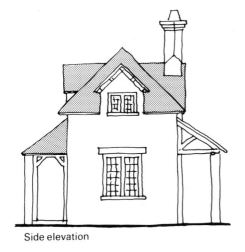

open shed

scullery

kitchen

pantry

seat

porch

Ground floor

The cottages are all similar in size and in the accommodation they provide, but they vary in their detailed design. The layout was carefully designed to produce a picturesque effect, and to ensure a degree of privacy for each tenant.

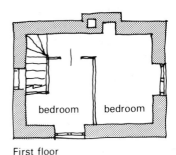

bedroom   bedroom

First floor

Side elevation

93

smaller farmers, many of whom lost their holdings in the open fields, and their grazing rights on the commons, and were forced to become landless labourers.

Throughout history the houses of these labourers, 'cottages' in the original sense of the word, had been of the poorest construction, many of them one-roomed hovels, few of which have survived. The changes of the later eighteenth century meant that still more people could afford to build houses only of this type. In many areas houses of these displaced farmers and other labourers were built on the wide verges of the turnpike roads, or on the edges of the still unenclosed heaths and commons. This 'squatting' may not have been strictly legal, but it was often condoned by the authorities. Rural poverty and squalor was becoming a national problem at the time when the large country house in its landscaped park had reached the finest stage of its development.

Until this period, small houses and cottages in rural areas had generally been built by their occupants, even though few of them were freeholders, many being copyholders or tenants at will. Now, probably as a direct result of the social effects of the agricultural revolution, we find a new development, that of cottages being built by landowners for their workers and

Eighteenth century ship-builders' cottages at Bucklers' Hard, Hampshire. A relic of a vanished industry.

Houses in Blaise Hamlet, Bristol. A 'model' estate of the early nineteenth century.

tenants, the 'model' or 'estate' cottages. This was to continue throughout the nineteenth century into the twentieth, when it was largely taken over by the Local Authorities.

Estate cottages were generally of a better standard than those the workers could have built for themselves, and many landowners clearly took their responsibilities seriously. It must be admitted, however, that this work was not always entirely altruistic. In the case of Milton Abbas in Dorset, the landowner, the Earl of Dorchester, completely demolished the old market town adjoining his house in order to lay out his new park. The displaced tenants were rehoused in an admittedly attractive 'model' village, built in an adjoining valley well out of sight of the house.

In other cases, model villages were designed on consciously picturesque lines to form an attractive approach to the large house. The gatehouses and lodges built at the entrances to the grounds were also often designed with this effect in mind as much as the welfare of the occupants.

Incidentally, it is in the estate cottages of the late eighteenth century that we first see the introduction of the semi-detached house. Not simply two houses built adjoining and attached to each other, but deliberately designed to look like one unit. This was to have a lasting effect on our towns and villages, particularly as the 'semi' came to be regarded as socially superior to the terrace.

An early Gothic Revival house at Totnes, Devon, probably c 1800.

The Gothic Revival

A desire for the picturesque was now to affect all classes of house. The classic Georgian style had lost some of its early inventiveness and had become increasingly standardized, partly, as we have seen, as a result of urban Building Acts and Regulations. In the second half of the eighteenth century a reaction set in — the Gothic Revival. This movement, inspired by contemporary literature, was at first rather light-hearted in character, and was not based on serious historical research. Pointed arches and other Gothic features were introduced into what were otherwise conventional Georgian houses. There was no attempt to return to a medieval house plan.

This fashion was accompanied by an interest in the ruins of abbeys and castles. Since the end of the Middle Ages these had been regarded as relics of a barbarian age, and treated with little respect, often having been used as quarries for building stone. Now they were considered desirable landscape features, and many owe their survival to this change in taste.

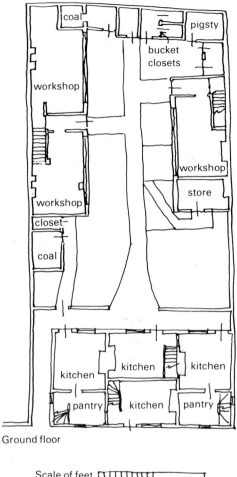

coal

pigsty

bucket closets

workshop

workshop

store

workshop

closet

coal

Ground floor

kitchen

kitchen

kitchen

kitchen

pantry

kitchen

pantry

Scale of feet

0   10   20

Fig. 32 **Ruddington framework knitters' shops and houses, Ruddington, Nottinghamshire. This complex of framework (hosiery) knitters' workshops and cottages was built in the early nineteenth century, when Nottingham and the surrounding villages became one of the main centres of this industry. The workshops, containing the knitting machines, were on two floors. The block of houses, consisting of two 'through' houses with two rooms on each floor, and two 'back-to-backs', with one room on each floor, each had two storeys and an attic. The owner occupied one of the larger houses, the others being occupied by some of his workers. Water for the whole complex was supplied from a pump in the central yard.**

This early industrial complex shows the relationship between the houses and the workshops, and indeed between the employer and his workers at this period. It is being restored and maintained as a museum.

Historical development:

Sometimes, however, these ruins were remodelled as landscape features with little regard for historical accuracy. Mock ruins and follies were also constructed at this period.

All this led, perhaps inevitably, to a more serious study of the past, and by the second quarter of the nineteenth century the Gothic Revival had changed in character. There was now a genuine attempt to copy medieval forms, and this can be seen in houses of all classes in the mid nineteenth century.

Urban growth

By the nineteenth century, too, there was a great increase in the growth of towns and in the movement of people into the towns from the rural areas. In the growing industrial towns this resulted in the building of large numbers of cheap houses to rent for the factory workers. The early nineteenth century slums were notorious and most of them have now disappeared, but in some towns a few of the 'back-to-back' houses are now being preserved as historical relics. Perhaps it is as well that they, and the circumstances which produced them, should not be forgotten.

Glodfa Ganol, Wales. Slate quarrymen's cottages. Welsh slate was widely used for roofing in the late eighteenth and nineteenth centuries. These primitive single-storey cottages show the survival of an early type into the nineteenth century.

Saltaire, West Yorkshire. A 'model' industrial village, built in the 1850s. One ground floor window retains its original glazing.

Some of the early industrialists, however, did build better houses for their workers, sometimes in the form of model estates, the urban equivalent of the model villages in rural areas. New Lanark, built by Robert Owen, a complete village with its factories and houses begun in the late eighteenth century is perhaps the best known of these. Saltaire, in West Yorkshire, is a later example, dating from the 1850s.

A growing awareness of the low standard of most industrial housing, and the diseases and other miseries arising from this, resulted in a movement to replace the slums with improved housing, often in the form of tenement blocks. These were generally provided by charitable trusts, and some of them still survive, looking to us almost as forbidding as the houses they replaced. Some real pioneer work was, however, done in this field,

99

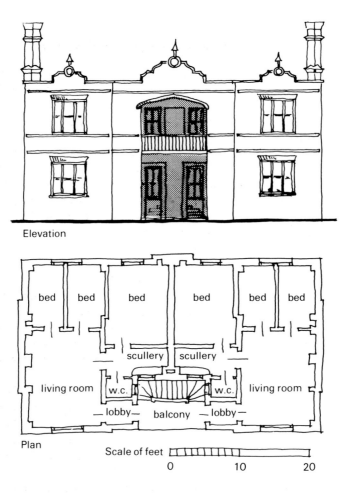

Elevation

Plan

Scale of feet

0   10   20

Fig. 33 **Prince Albert Lodge, London. This block of four flats was originally erected at the Great Exhibition of 1851 as an example of improved working class housing. It was designed by H. Roberts for the Society for Improving the Condition of the Labouring Classes. The Prince Consort, the President of the Society, took an interest in the design. The accommodation provided was probably considerably better than that enjoyed by most of the urban working class at the time. It is significant that two bedrooms, albeit very small, were provided for the children in each family. Victorian reformers were stressing the need for separate bedrooms for children of each sex.**

There were a number of unusual features in this building. Hollow bricks were used, not only for the walls, but for the first floor and roof construction, avoiding the use of timber. The first floor and roof were of arched construction, tied with wrought iron rods, the arches being levelled off with concrete. The design was repeated in a few other places, including Stepney, Kensington, and Hertford. The modified Tudor style of the building was to influence subsequent Victorian houses of all classes, evolving into the popular Queen Anne style of the latter part of the nineteenth century.

This building was re-erected in Kennington Park, South London, in 1852, to be used to house two park attendants and a museum of 'Articles relating to cottage economy'.

100

particularly that inspired by Prince Albert. A block of urban tenements, reputedly designed under his guidance and constructed for the Great Exhibition of 1851, has been rebuilt in Kennington Park, South London, and it is an interesting example of enlightened Victorian thinking on artisan housing (fig. 33).

The prince's own death from typhoid, and the outbreaks of cholera in the later nineteenth century, demonstrated the need for improvements in water supply and drainage, and in these and other matters increased public control over town planning and building brought about a progressive improvement in urban living conditions. The Public Health Act of 1875 required Local Authorities in Britain to make bye-laws regulating the construction and spacing of houses.

At a higher social level more building, much of it speculative, for sale or rent, took place in the towns and suburbs in the nineteenth century. Terraces which had been socially acceptable in the eighteenth century declined in popularity, probably because of their association with working-class housing. Better-class houses were now more often detached or semi-detached. Only in comparatively recent times has the terrace house come back into favour.

In the later nineteenth century there was a general movement from the town centres to the suburbs by all who could afford this. As a result, many of the older, larger, town houses were divided into tenements and their gardens built over. In this way many fine houses deteriorated and have been demolished as slums, often without their true interest and value being realised until too late.

Architecturally, early nineteenth century houses still showed the influence of the classic Georgian style, although they were generally plainer. Later in the century, particularly after the Great Exhibition of 1851, domestic architecture was influenced not only by the Gothic Revival, but by some of the foreign styles popularised by the exhibits at Hyde Park.

Towards the end of the century a new influence was felt, affecting both urban and rural housing. This was the Arts and Crafts movement, an offshoot of the Gothic Revival, which led to the Vernacular Revival. It was inspired by the writings and work of William Morris, and of such architects as Philip Webb, Norman Shaw and Charles Voysey, and was an attempt to return to a traditional way of building, rejecting both the classical formality of the Renaissance and the ostentation of some of the Victorian styles. It was paralleled by the Pre-Raphaelite movement in painting.

Some of the buildings inspired by this movement may appear rather

Housing at Hampstead Garden Suburb, a conscious revival of the vernacular tradition. Although they were built as long ago as 1910, houses such as these influenced domestic design until after the Second World War.

self-conscious to us today, particularly those most influenced by Art Nouveau, an offshoot of the original style. There is no doubt, however, about its lasting effect on house design. The still popular traditional cottage style is a direct result of this movement, which was concerned not only with the design of individual houses but with their layout and setting. The 'Garden Suburbs', of which Bedford Park in West London was the first, and Hampstead perhaps the most well known, were followed by the more ambitious Garden Cities of Letchworth and Welwyn, inspired by the writings of Ebenezer Howard. Similar developments such as Bourneville and Port Sunlight were created by large industrial concerns for their workers, and Local Authority housing schemes have reflected the same influence, which can still be seen in many present-day housing layouts.

Recent developments

In towns, there has recently been a return to higher density development and to the residential use of town centres — a reversal of previous trends.

Some of the larger town houses are being converted into good quality flats, and new terraced 'town houses' are becoming popular. Often, to make the best use of expensive town sites, these houses are planned with garages and utility rooms on the ground floor, with living accommodation above — a return to medieval ideas of town living.

In the immediate post-war years high rise blocks of flats were favoured, particularly for Local Authority housing, but more recently there has been a reaction in favour of smaller scale development, reflecting a desire for a more human and intimate environment. New terraces and smaller blocks of flats are being built, and some of the nineteenth century terraces of smaller houses which had escaped wholesale demolition and redevelopment are being modernized and up-graded.

While the Garden City movement, which influenced much of the planning of the earlier post-war New Towns, raised the general standard of housing, it tended to abandon the older town centres to decay or commercial development. Today we are seeing a revival of the town centre itself as a desirable place to live, in an essentially urban (not suburban) setting.

In rural areas the position is perhaps less hopeful. With a few notable exceptions, most new housing in villages seems to take the form of estates planned on low-density suburban lines, and it is difficult to see how these will ever be integrated visually with the old village centres.

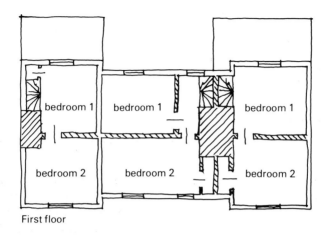

First floor

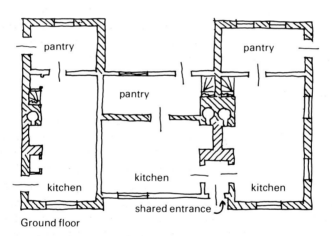

Ground floor

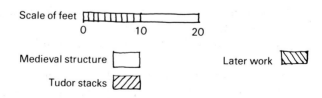

Scale of feet

0   10   20

Medieval structure

Tudor stacks

Later work

Fig 34 **Conversion of a Wealden farmhouse into three cottages in the eighteenth or nineteenth century.**

5
Changes in status and function

In rural areas most smaller and medium sized houses were built by farmers of various classes, and others engaged in agriculture. In the towns most houses in the earlier periods were built by merchants, shopkeepers and tradesmen, and later also by members of the professional classes and those employed in commerce and industry. The social status of a house, however, does not necessarily remain the same. Houses may move up and down in the social scale. Some houses were built for particular purposes which have changed or died out. Certain non-residential buildings have been adapted as houses when their original use ceased.

Farmhouses

Let us start by looking again at the farmhouse. As we have seen, at the time of the Parliamentary Enclosures, when new farmhouses were built out in the enclosed fields, many of the old houses in the village street were converted into cottages for farmworkers. Often, too, the old barns in the village were similarly converted, sometimes rather roughly and as cheaply as possible, and in some cases it will be found that rooms on the first floor of one cottage are above ground floor rooms in the adjoining one, a feature known as a 'flying freehold'. This conversion of redundant houses and barns was a cheaper alternative to the building of special dwellings, the model cottages being put up by the larger landowners. It was another outcome of the social changes of the age.

In the case of the old farmhouses, much of the original character of the house was masked as a result of this treatment and this, combined with a lower standard of maintenance, resulted in a general deterioration in its status and condition, often leading to demolition. Many such houses, their historic value not appreciated until too late, have been destroyed as part of a slum clearance programme, as happened in the towns.

The process, however, did not always end in this way. In recent years,

Changes in status and function

due to a growing interest in old houses, and perhaps to the increase in second homes, many of these old farmhouses have been bought for restoration by new owners. Sometimes, indeed, this followed the condemnation and closing of the converted cottages by the Local Authority, and the rehousing of the tenants in Council houses.

Not only have larger farmhouses been bought and rehabilitated in this way, but quite small cottages have been bought as retirement or weekend homes by people of a very different class from those for whom they were built. Barns, too, are now being converted into houses of quite a high social status, a process very different in spirit from their utilitarian conversion in the late eighteenth and nineteenth centuries. In recent years, specialized buildings such as the traditional Kentish oast houses, superseded for their original purpose by more modern hop-drying kilns, have been popular subjects for residential conversion.

Quarrymen's and fishermen's cottages at Lamorna Cove, Cornwall, in process of conversion to 'quality' (probably holiday) cottages.

Saffron Walden, Essex. An old farmhouse in the village street, converted into cottages, probably following the enclosures of the eighteenth century.

A Victorian conversion of an oast house at Meopham, Kent.

Eighteenth century hunt kennels at Iwerne Steepleton, Dorset, later converted into cottages.

Town houses

When we turn to town houses we may find a similar cycle of social change. Most medieval and Tudor houses in the centres of towns were used for commercial as well as residential purposes. The ground floor front room was a shop or a workshop. Behind was the hall, with the counting house, office and warehouses beyond this. The other living accommodation was on the upper floors. Sometimes the hall extended through two floors. By the late seventeenth and eighteenth centuries we find town houses built purely for residential use, their occupants working elsewhere. At a later date many of these houses have been converted for shop use, with shop fronts inserted and the ground floor largely remodelled. In most cases, however, the upper floors were still in residential use — the tradesman lived 'over the shop'.

More recently still this has changed again, partly because of the growth of multiple firms at the expense of the private trader, and upper floors of shops are now often used only for storage, and as a result their condition deteriorates. Sometimes the upper floors are let off as offices, but for this use as well as for continued or revived residential use, modern building and fire regulations are creating considerable difficulties.

Both in towns and to a lesser extent in rural areas, large houses have been converted to offices or for institutional purposes, and this trend is continuing for houses which, because of their size or their situation, are no longer finding a ready market for residential use. However, the trends are not all in one direction. Some large houses, and even the stables and coachhouses in the mews courts, are being converted into flats.

So far we have been considering houses that were originally built for normal residential use, combined in rural areas with farming, and in towns with retail trade. There are, however, other classes of building which we may now find being used as private houses, although this was not their main or only original function.

Crafts and industries

In rural areas not everyone was employed in agriculture. Every village had its craftsmen, whose houses incorporated their workshops. In most cases the craft use has ceased, but the houses may still show evidence of it.

After farming the most important rural trade was probably milling. Watermills and windmills were known in medieval times, although most surviving examples date from the eighteenth and nineteenth centuries. There was usually a mill house adjoining the mill itself, and this has generally survived, the mill either having been demolished or incorporated into the house. Sometimes part of the machinery remains. Sometimes the mill stream and pond provide evidence of the original function of the building. Many more watermills than windmills have been converted into houses and today watermills in particular are being converted into 'prestige' houses, with much of the machinery deliberately preserved. Mills were often manorial property, and referred to in manorial records — some are mentioned in the Domesday Book. Such records, of course, only verify that there was a mill on the site at a particular date, they cannot be used to date an existing structure.

The wheelwright and the smith were both important craftsmen in pre-industrial times. Their workshops usually adjoined their houses, and in some cases have survived either as outbuildings or incorporated into the house. Sometimes the original function of the building is commemorated in the house name, or may be traced from early maps.

In areas where the cloth industry flourished spinning and weaving were important cottage industries, in some places lasting into the industrial age

Late eighteenth century weavers' houses at Golcar, West Yorkshire. The long windows on the upper floor lit the weaving rooms.

when work was still put out to outworkers. Houses of spinners and weavers are often distinguished by large rooms, generally on an upper floor, with long horizontal windows to provide the necessary daylight for the looms. In some areas, such as the Lake District, there was a special open spinning gallery. In many cases these rooms have now been incorporated into the main living area of the house.

Another category of house which had a subsidiary business use was the toll house. These little houses were built in conjunction with the construction of the Turnpike roads in the late eighteenth and early nineteenth centuries, and are found close to the roadside (a fact which has made them very susceptible to demolition for road-widening schemes). They often have quite a distinctive character: they may be octagonal or hexagonal in plan, with windows in the canted walls, or have large bay windows to provide good visibility along the road. Many of them were specially built by the Turnpike Trusts, and were designed in a uniform style, often of Tudor or early Gothic Revival character. A similar type of building is the lock-keeper's cottage found on the canals. These were often

Thorn House, Hartsop, Cumbria. A seventeenth century Lakeland farmhouse with an open spinners' gallery.

A toll house at Motcombe, Dorset. The ground floor windows in the projecting bay (some since blocked) gave a good view of approaching traffic on the Turnpike Road.

built by the canal companies in a uniform style. Still in the field of transport, we must not forget the early railway houses. The older stations incorporated a Station Master's house, and terraces of cottages were built by the railway companies for other workers. As the smaller stations are being closed, some of them are now being converted for other purposes, including housing. In the case of all these 'transport' buildings, the records of the company which built them may well survive, and can assist in tracing their history.

Charitable and religious foundations

The almshouse, or almshouse group, is a feature of many towns and villages. This is a building type with an interesting history going back to the

An almshouse group at Harefield, Middlesex, built in 1600 by the Countess of Derby; the successor to the medieval hospice and forerunner of the Old Persons' Homes of today. The windows may have been blocked to deaden noise from the road.

Nineteenth century canal-workers' houses at Tyrley Wharf, Staffordshire.

Middle Ages. At this time the hospital, or hospice, generally run by a religious order, cared both for the temporarily ill and the old and incapacitated. The typical plan was similar to that of a church, the nave being the 'ward' or living area for the inhabitants, and the chancel the hospital chapel. Some buildings of this type still survive, used for their original purpose, including Saint Mary's Hospital, Chichester, and the Almshouse of Saints John the Evangelist and John the Baptist, Sherborne.

After the Reformation most of the 'hospitals' were dissolved, but many were subsequently re-founded, this time usually as almshouses for the old people of the parish who had no relatives to care for them. In place of the communal medieval plan, the new almshouses were built as a series of individual units, generally with a Warden's house and perhaps a chapel. These groups can be very attractive, and almshouses of this type continued to be built and rebuilt into the nineteenth century. Many are still in use today, but some have been replaced with more modern accommodation and converted to new uses. Occasionally they have been adapted as private houses, and this trend may increase. It is interesting that almshouses often seem to have been built in an architectural style which was rather old-fashioned at the time of their building. They often have date-stones and the

113

Bury St Edmunds, Suffolk. In the eighteenth and nineteenth centuries houses were actually built into the ruined west wall of the former Abbey Church.

charity owning them probably has good written records, so their history is relatively easy to trace.

Apart from the almshouses founded by private individuals or religious or charitable trusts, we may find a 'poor house' provided by the Parish; before the changes in the Poor Law in 1834 resulted in the building of the larger Union Workhouses. A number of the earlier, smaller Poor Houses have been sold by the parishes and are now private houses. The Parish Records should be able to help in dating these. There is not necessarily anything architecturally to distinguish these buildings from normal houses of the same date.

Almshouses were not, of course, the only buildings left by the religious orders. At the dissolution of the religious houses the monastic buildings passed into secular ownership. Many were demolished, but others were adapted for new uses, often as private houses. Usually the domestic buildings of the monastery were converted in this way, but occasionally the church itself was adapted, as at Buckland Abbey in Devon, and Titchfield

114

Buckland Abbey, Devon. The Church of a Cistercian Abbey converted into a house, subsequently the home of Sir Francis Drake.

Abbey in Hampshire. Sometimes the conversion was carried out on a grand scale, as at Forde Abbey in Dorset, but at other times it seems to have been done on a purely utilitarian basis, with little respect for the original fabric. This could produce some interesting results, as at Bury St Edmunds in Suffolk, where houses were inserted into the ruins of the west wall of the Abbey Church.

Today a number of redundant churches of all denominations are being converted into houses. This was not unknown in the past. Generally the ecclesiastical origin of the building is fairly obvious, and we have to consider not only the date of the original church but the date of its conversion into a house. This will lead to investigation of the reason the church fell into disuse. The population of the parish may have been wiped out by an outbreak of plague or other disease, or a change from arable to sheep farming could result in areas being depopulated. In other cases the community may have failed to survive for economic reasons; it may have been established during a time of population growth on poor soil, and been abandoned when the population shrank. At the time of the Reformation a number of pilgrim chapels were closed. Sometimes, as we have seen, a village was deliberately removed by a landowner to create a park, with a few houses or other buildings left as landscape features. In more recent times churches have been closed following the amalgamation of parishes, both in towns and in rural areas.

It is sometimes said of an old house, particularly one in a village, that it was once a chapel, although there may be nothing about its design to suggest this. It must be remembered that in the early days of Non-conformity, and particularly at the start of the Methodist movement, the small community met at the houses of their leading members. Such a house might come to be known as 'the Chapel', and remain in use as such until the increased congregation justified the provision of a purpose-built chapel in the area. If the records of the local branch of the denomination have survived some light may be thrown on this phase in the history of the house concerned.

Many smaller schools, particularly in villages, have been closed and their buildings sold. Quite often the old school is converted into a house, perhaps incorporating the former school house. The records of the school, whether it was run by the Church, the Parish or Town, or a private charity, should be available, and will probably provide a date for the building or rebuilding of the property.

The Old Grammar School, Chard, Somerset, now converted to a private house.

This process of social change is a continuing one and many old buildings owe their survival to an adaptation to a new use. Sometimes the necessary conversion is carried out in a strictly utilitarian manner, with little respect for the character of the building. At other times we find rather a self-conscious over-restoration, which can be equally damaging. When, however, the work is carried out sensitively and imaginatively it can give the building a worthwhile new lease of life, and provide a very attractive house.

A seventeenth-century inn in Worcester, with an inserted Edwardian ground floor. Despite the contrast in style, the overall effect is quite harmonious.

6
Travellers' houses: the Inn

Socially and architecturally the inn has played an important part in towns and villages since medieval times. Many old inns have well-known historical and literary associations (some more apocryphal than real) which add to their popularity. In recent years, however, many old inns have closed to be sold as private houses, and this trend is increasing in some areas. Anyone buying a former inn will want to learn something of its history — as distinct from popular local legend — and this interest may also be shared by those who patronise inns as 'regulars' or visitors.

In trying to discover the history of an inn, or former inn, the documentary sources mentioned in Chapter 1 should all be investigated. In addition, more information may be obtainable from the alehouse recognisences, early forerunners of the licensing system which date from the seventeenth century onwards, and from the licences in the Quarter Sessions. These may all be available for study in the local Record Office.

The Church House at Braunton, Devon, now a village museum.

Travellers' houses

If the inn belongs, or belonged, to one of the larger breweries this may have some information both of the early history of the inn and of later alterations. It must be remembered that the names of inns were sometimes changed, perhaps to commemorate an important national event or a new monarch.

On the Tithe Maps the smaller alehouses may be described simply as 'cottages'. In such cases, by checking the name of the occupier in the appropriate census return, which will give his occupation (e.g. Innkeeper, or Beerseller), it will be possible to verify whether an inn, or a reputed former inn, was in use as such at the time the Tithe Map was prepared. From this point it may be possible to work back through the licensing records, or the alehouse recognisences, to trace preceding occupants and, perhaps, changes in the name of the inn.

The inn as we know it seems to have had two distinct origins in the Middle Ages, both having some connection with the Church. The first was the alehouse or tavern, built for the sale of ale and other liquor, and the second was the hostel for travellers. The alehouse may be considered the successor to the wine shop of Roman times. Indeed, the green bush hung outside the Roman wine shop to indicate its trade was the forerunner of the later inn sign. These alehouses must have existed in all the medieval towns, most of them being secular and commercial in origin, and fulfilling the same function as their modern successors. In plan they were probably not unlike the normal medieval town houses, the hall being the communal eating and drinking area.

In some towns and villages, however, while alehouses and taverns of this type certainly existed in the Middle Ages, they had to compete with the Church, since the brewing and selling of 'Church Ales' was a recognised means of increasing the Church's income, rather like the church fete or bazaar of today, and this was one of the responsibilities of the church-wardens. At first the church ale was probably sold from temporary booths set up in the churchyard, but by the later Middle Ages a Church House was often built adjoining or near the churchyard. It served also as a centre for the social activities of the parish. Most of the surviving examples are in the West Country. As far as can be seen, allowing for later alterations, the typical Church House had a large first-floor room approached by an external staircase, and a series of smaller rooms, stores and service rooms, on the ground floor. At Sherborne, Dorset, the ground floor room of the Church House seems always to have been divided into shops, as at present, and this may have been usual in towns, providing additional revenue for the Church.

The Church House, Sherborne, Dorset. The upper floor originally consisted of one long room. The ground floor probably always comprised shops, as at present.

The Church House, at Manaton, Devon, now private houses looking directly on to the churchyard.

Travellers' houses

After the Reformation, because of Puritan disapproval, the brewing of church ales was stopped and the Church Houses which were not destroyed were converted to other uses, often as private houses. The one at Crowcombe, Somerset, became an almshouse, but it has recently been converted to a church hall, regaining something of its original function. In a few cases the Church House actually became a secular alehouse, the village inn. More often, a new inn was built on or near the old site, explaining why the village inn is so often near the church.

Until the nineteenth century most brewing was carried out locally, and some old inns still have their former brewhouses and malt houses, now probably used as outbuildings, beer stores or garages. Old malt houses are sometimes converted for residential use, but the low storey heights in many of these buildings can present problems when this is done.

It is difficult to trace any typical plan forms for the early village alehouse or inn, as they have been altered continually over the centuries to suit changing tastes and needs. Another problem is that by no means all existing inns were built for this purpose. Many are former farmhouses or cottages. In any case, innkeeping was not always a full-time occupation. The innkeeper might well depend partly, even mainly, on farming or a trade for his living.

The smaller 'locals', the successors to the early alehouses and taverns, increased greatly in number in the eighteenth and nineteenth centuries, particularly in the growing industrial towns. Here they eventually acquired a distinctive style, Baroque in inspiration, featuring glazed tiles, polished mahogany and engraved glass. The association of this 'gin palace' style with the evils resulting from drunkenness, which gave rise to the later nineteenth century temperance movements, has perhaps been responsible for the replacement of this 'pub' style with a more neutral one in the present century.

Another result of the industrial revolution was the building of canalside inns to serve the boatmen. These had a commercial as well as a purely social function. The self-employed boatmen, the 'Number ones', could meet potential customers and arrange for cargo deliveries. Moorings were provided by the inn, which acted as an exchange for news and messages between the boatmen. The Swan, at Fradley Junction, on the Trent and Mersey Canal, is a good example. At certain inns, stabling was provided for the canal horses. With the decline of the canals due to competition from the railways many of these inns disappeared, or were converted to other uses, but they are now enjoying a revival with the growing use of the canals for pleasure boating.

The Red Lion Inn, Southampton. This fifteenth century building was probably originally a merchant's house. The pseudo-Tudor exterior hides an authentic medieval open hall.

If the primary function of the alehouse or tavern was to sell ale, the need to provide accommodation for travellers was first supplied, in medieval times, by the religious houses. Many of the religious orders had a rule that no bona-fide traveller could be refused a meal and a bed for the night, and they often had guest houses. Those religious houses situated on busy routes and in popular pilgrim centres must have found that this provision of hospitality interfered with the normal routine of the Order, and this led to the building of hostels or inns, separate from the Abbey in the towns or on the main roads. Other inns of this type were built and run by private landlords as business concerns, their numbers increasing as more settled conditions and the growth of trade brought an increase in the numbers of travellers.

'Pilgrims at an Inn', from MS.Hunter 252, late fifteenth century. Ten to a room, shared beds and lack of privacy were common in these early inns.

Some of these medieval inns have survived, notably the Pilgrims' Inn (now The George) at Glastonbury, Somerset (fig. 35), The Angel at Grantham, Lincolnshire, and The George at Norton St Philip, Somerset (fig. 36). As with the early alehouses, it is difficult to determine the original plan form, because of the many later alterations, but it would appear that the main sleeping accommodation was of a communal dormitory character, reflecting the usual monastic arrangements. Only the more wealthy travellers would be provided with private rooms. Apart from this, the plan probably resembled that of the typical late medieval town house, the courtyard plan being popular for the larger inns.

After the Reformation the running of all hostels and inns passed into secular hands. As with the alehouses, a reminder of their religious origin

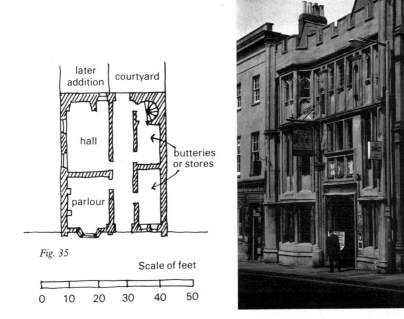

Fig. 35

later addition | courtyard

hall

butteries or stores

parlour

Scale of feet

0 10 20 30 40 50

The George Inn, Glastonbury, Somerset; built in the fifteenth century by the monks of Glastonbury Abbey for the many pilgrims who came here in the Middle Ages. The high quality of the building indicates the great wealth of the Abbey. It would probably have been flanked by timber-framed buildings.

survives in the character of many of their signs. Some of these are obvious: the Cross Keys of Saint Peter and the Lamb and Flag of Saint John the Baptist are easy to recognise. Fewer people would realise that 'Peter's Finger' is probably a corruption of Saint Peter ad Vincula (Saint Peter in Chains). On the other hand, some inn signs are of pagan, pre-christian origin, such as The Green Man or Jack in the Green.

When sleeping accommodation came to be provided in smaller rooms instead of in communal dormitories, open galleries were often constructed at the upper floor levels to provide access to these rooms. This was becoming normal practice by the sixteenth century, and it was particularly well suited to timber-framed construction. In more recent times many of these galleries have been enclosed with solid walls or with glazing, but traces of the old construction can sometimes be seen.

By the late sixteenth century, with a continuing increase in the numbers

125

The George, Norton St Philip, Somerset, built and run by the monks of Hinton Charterhouse to provide accommodation for pilgrims and other travellers. The photograph, taken in the courtyard, shows the staircase tower, as seen in the plan (below).

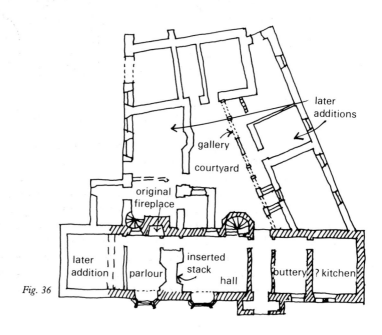

Fig. 36

later additions

gallery

courtyard

original fireplace

later addition

parlour

inserted stack

hall

buttery

? kitchen

The White Hart Hotel, Romsey, Hampshire. A Georgian facade hides an earlier galleried courtyard. The galleries have since been enclosed.

of travellers on the roads, the inns were growing in importance. They were already being used as 'Posting Houses' supplying changes of horses, and their standards of food and accommodation were improving. By the early seventeenth century the first stage coaches appeared, providing the first real public transport and bringing regular custom to the inns. This trade developed throughout the eighteenth century and reached its height in the early nineteenth century. By that time improvements in road construction made it possible for the coaches to run to strict timetables, and the main inns along the coaching routes had a coaching office where bookings could be made. In many cases, the inns were owned by the coaching companies.

Travellers' houses

When the coach arrived at the inn the richer travellers could hire private dining rooms, while those less well off dined in a common room or hall and servants and others of inferior rank might have to eat in the kitchen. In the meantime the horses were changed, and fresh postilions took over for the next stage of the journey.

In addition to this regular stage coach traffic, there were the faster mail coaches, and private travellers using their own carriages or hired post-chaises. There were also the carriers transporting goods between towns, and as a result of this increased trade many of the older inns were rebuilt or enlarged. The courtyard plan was still popular, although the open galleries had by now been abandoned. The larger inns had two courtyards. Round the main courtyard, approached from the street through an archway, were the entrance hall, the dining rooms, coffee room, the coach office, and the main bedrooms on the upper floors; beyond this was the rear courtyard, surrounded by the kitchens, service rooms and stables, with the servants' rooms above them.

One social change which affected the external appearance of the inn was the growing popularity, in the later eighteenth century, of travelling 'outside' or on the top of the coach. This meant that the entrance archways had to be raised, and it is possible in some inns to see where this has been done.

The original plans of many of these coaching inns have been altered in more recent times, but it may be possible to trace the earlier layout and arrangement of rooms. In particular, from the nineteenth century onwards, the open courtyards were sometimes completely roofed in, often with glass, so that their original form is not immediately apparent except, perhaps, for the large entrance archway which may have been partly blocked to take a normal-sized door.

When the development of the railways put an end to the stage coach services the inns lost much of their trade. Some survived, but others were demolished or converted to other uses, including private houses. New hotels and inns appeared, however, to serve the railway stations, many of them built by the railway companies, who often favoured a revived Gothic style. The interiors of these railway hotels could be quite impressive, and it is perhaps unfortunate that their character is only now beginning to be appreciated when so many of them have been drastically altered.

By the late nineteenth century a new development helped to save and revive some of the older inns. People were beginning to travel for pleasure, and not just as a necessity. Walking tours became popular, and the invention of the bicycle, followed by that of the motor car, brought

The Duke's Head Hotel, King's Lynn, Norfolk. A wealthy merchant's house of the late seventeenth century, designed by Henry Bell, and later converted to a coaching inn.

renewed trade to the inns. The disused stables were converted to garages, or to additional accommodation, and new forms of inn such as the Motel have appeared to meet the new demands.

As more people in all walks of life were given paid holidays, provision was made for longer-stay guests as well as for overnight travellers. New inns and hotels were built catering for this type of trade, particularly in the developing holiday resorts.

All these developments have affected the old inns, both the local alehouses and the larger hotels. Many of them have been bought by the large breweries, who have spent a great deal of money on them, in some cases changing their character considerably. In addition to this general refurbishment, much of the work needed to comply with the requirements of the Licensing and Fire Authorities has had quite a drastic effect on the character of old inns and hotels. Change is perhaps inevitable, and when it is a genuine reflection of the changing needs of the age it can add to the historic interest of a building. In the case of the inn, however, much of the present refurbishment seems designed to give the building rather a bogus historic character. Even more often than in private houses we will find 'old oak beams' that not only have no structural function, but may even be made of fibreglass. It seems sad that the inn, with its long history and robust traditions, should feel the need to adopt this spurious antiquity.

7
Historical survey of a house. The exterior

Having studied the development of the house and some of its variations, it is time to look in detail at individual buildings. The first thing to note is the siting of the house. Is it in a town or a village street, in a small hamlet group, or isolated in a rural area? If in a street, is it part of a planned terrace, all apparently of one build? Does it appear to be part of a larger building, now sub-divided? How does it compare in size, apparent age and general character with adjoining or nearby houses?

Most towns started as comparatively small settlements and spread outwards. The oldest buildings are therefore likely to be in the centre, near the parish church and the market place. Outer suburbs were generally developed later, although sometimes old villages were absorbed into them and retain some old houses. London is a good example of this.

In a village, too, the oldest houses are likely to be near the centre. On the outskirts we may find examples of highway verge encroachment. The shape of the house plots may also help us. The medieval farmhouses in the village street generally had fairly narrow plots running back from the street frontage, sometimes extending to a 'back lane'. Later cottages built on the highway verges have wider, shallower plots, running parallel to the road.

An isolated farmhouse may be of early, perhaps Tudor, origin, if it is in an area where the farming pattern was one of small enclosures rather than the open field system. A clue to this may be found in the field pattern. The fields round the house are likely to be small and irregular in shape. In an area where the open field system was in operation, and not enclosed until the eighteenth century, the isolated farms probably date from this period. Here the fields will be larger and more regular in shape. Today, of course, this pattern is being changed by the removal of hedges and the

Houses in Bury St Edmunds, Suffolk. The timber-framing has been plastered externally, and sash windows inserted in the eighteenth century, but the surviving jetty indicates their original construction. The roofs would originally have been thatched or tiled. Slates would not have been used here before the eighteenth century.

131

A house in Abbots Bromley, Staffordshire, showing a Georgian brick facade applied to an earlier timber-framed house, revealed in the end wall.

amalgamation of fields, but the old pattern may still be traced, or checked from the early 1:2500 Ordnance Survey maps.

In towns a clue to the age of the houses is sometimes given by the street names, particularly from the eighteenth century onwards. A good example of this is seen in the Esplanade area of Weymouth, Dorset, which was developed after King George III's visits made the town fashionable as a resort. The Esplanade developed northwards and southwards from Gloucester Lodge, built in 1780 and where the King stayed. The names of the terraces, such as Gloucester Row built in 1790, Royal Crescent in 1805, Royal Terrace in 1816–20, Waterloo Place in 1830, and Victoria Terrace in 1855, tell the story of the progressive development of the Esplanade.

In more recent times, names such as Jubilee Terrace and Coronation Square can tell their own story, although we should remember that buildings and streets may be re-named at a later date.

Next we should look at the house itself starting with the exterior,

132

although by now it will be clear that this, particularly the front elevation, may be later than the main structure. It is as well to look at the back of the house if we can — it is not always easy in a town — as this is less likely than the front to have been refaced. With a free-standing building, a close inspection may reveal the fact that the main facade has been rebuilt.

Let us assume that our house is free-standing, or at least that most of the exterior is visible. The first thing to note is the general shape of the building. Until the eighteenth century most smaller houses were only one room deep. After this period the double-pile plan became popular. If the house is two or more rooms deep, does this appear to be the original form, or a later alteration? An examination of the end walls will often make this clear.

Note also if the front and rear walls appear to have been raised, and the roof pitch flattened, in order to give more headroom on the top floor. This was frequently done to older houses in the eighteenth and nineteenth centuries. It can often be seen on the end gable wall, and sometimes a change of material can be seen in the top section of the front and rear walls. Sometimes this raising was done at the front of the house only, the old eaves line and roof pitch surviving unaltered at the rear.

Stafford Park Farm, Puddletown, Dorset. A single-pile house later increased to two rooms in depth and given a new low-pitched roof. The original depth of this house can clearly be seen in the masonry on the end wall.

The gable end of a cruck house at Much Wenlock, Shropshire. The front
and rear walls have been raised to increase headroom on the upper floor.

If the main elevation is symmetrical, this suggests a date no earlier than
the late seventeenth century for the building. However, as well as looking
at the positions of the windows and doors, those of the chimney stacks
should also be noted. Are they also symmetrical? If not, the facade may
well be a remodelling of an older building. It is relatively easy to reface a
building, but less easy to re-site large old chimney stacks.

134

Note also whether or not the whole house appears to be of one build, or whether the original building has been extended. Sometimes an added section is easy to identify: there may be a change of walling material; the architectural style of the windows, etc., may be later; the roof may be at a different level, or pitch. In other cases the addition may be less obvious, but close inspection may reveal a change in the character of the walling even if the same basic material was used: there may be a straight joint between the two sections, or the bonding of the newer work to the older may be obvious. Sometimes a feature of the original building, for instance a plinth or a string course, may not be continued round the newer section.

Next, note the materials used for the external walls. Were they obtained locally? Normally, except for large and important buildings, materials were not transported for long distances until the coming of cheap transport by canal, rail or modern roads. For smaller houses local materials were used, and we will now look at these in turn.

This Wealden house at Cowden, Kent, has suffered several changes. The outer wall of the hall and the ground floor walls of the end blocks have been rebuilt in brick, doing away with the jetties and creating a flush facade. The end wall has been weatherboarded. In spite of this the original form of the house can still be traced.

135

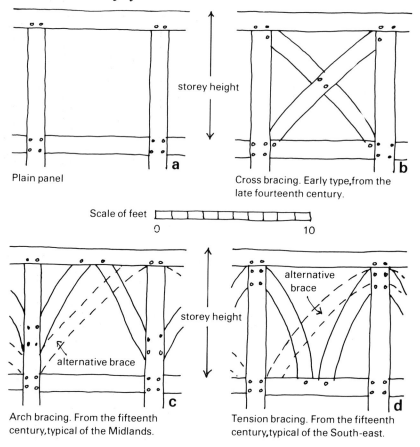

Plain panel

a

Cross bracing. Early type, from the late fourteenth century.

b

Scale of feet

0   10

Arch bracing. From the fifteenth century, typical of the Midlands.

c

alternative brace

Tension bracing. From the fifteenth century, typical of the South-east.

d

alternative brace

Fig. 37 **Timber-framing, large panel type. Probably the earliest form of timber-framing, found in all areas by the mid fifteenth century. After c 1500 it is usually found only in poorer-class houses and the less important facades of better houses. Less common after the mid sixteenth century.**

Timber-framing

This was the usual material for small and medium sized houses from medieval times, in all areas where good timber was available. One problem of dating timber-framed buildings is the ease with which they may be altered. They were also at times taken down and rebuilt, sometimes on a different site, and in an altered form.

There is little evidence of surviving timber-framed houses dating from

136

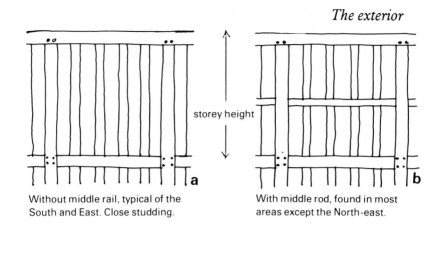

Without middle rail, typical of the South and East. Close studding. **a**

With middle rod, found in most areas except the North-east. **b**

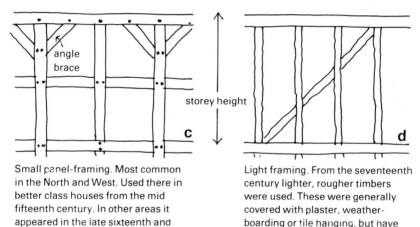

Small panel-framing. Most common in the North and West. Used there in better class houses from the mid fifteenth century. In other areas it appeared in the late sixteenth and seventeenth centuries in small houses **c**

Light framing. From the seventeenth century lighter, rougher timbers were used. These were generally covered with plaster, weatherboarding or tile hanging, but have sometimes been exposed in recent restorations. **d**

Fig. 38 **Timber-framing, later forms.**

before the fourteenth century, and not many surviving examples are earlier than the fifteenth century. Most of these early houses were relatively good class buildings, homes of yeomen, merchants and people of higher status. In the early houses the timbers were generally framed together to form large panels, with various forms of diagonal bracing (fig. 37). The roofs were often supported by crucks, and this may sometimes be seen in the end gable walls.

House at Market Drayton, Shropshire, showing the highly ornamental framing typical of the north-west.

Moat Farm, Dormston, Hereford and Worcestershire. Small panel timber-framing. The gabled dormers are later insertions. The pentice weatherings protected the walling below from rain running down the wall face.

Bunyan's Mead, Elstow, Bedfordshire. Close studding with ornamental curved braces. The carriage entrance is believed to have led to an inn yard.

Historical survey of a house: The exterior

Timber-framing in smaller panels is first seen from the mid fifteenth century in the north and west of Britain, where it began to replace the large panel framing in the larger and better-class houses (fig. 38c). In other areas it appeared rather later, generally in smaller houses. In the North and West, this small panel framing developed into various ornamental patterns, and this fashion continued into the seventeenth century.

Timber-framing with closely spaced vertical studs (fig. 38a) generally dates from after about 1500, and was most popular in the South-east.

Both these later types were more expensive than the earlier large panel framing, using a greater proportion of timber, and they are normally found in houses built by the comparatively wealthy. Indeed, in the same building we may find large panel framing used in the less important parts, such as the back wall, and the more expensive forms in the front wall. This does not necessarily indicate different dates for the different parts of the house.

By the seventeenth century small panel framing, without ornamental patterning, was the normal construction for smaller houses in all areas, replacing the large panel framing. In the North and West the larger houses were built with highly ornamental panel framing. Little Moreton Hall, Cheshire, is a good example of this. In the South-east close vertical studding was still in use, but by this time, in this area, brick was beginning to replace timber-framing in houses whose owners could afford this new material.

From the seventeenth century onwards some houses were being built with rougher, lighter timbers (fig. 38d), generally plastered externally. The timbers in these houses were not intended to be seen. In some cases they have been mistakenly stripped in recent restorations. Sometimes, the plaster covering was modelled to produce a decorative effect. Plant forms and geometrical designs were popular. This treatment is most often found in East Anglia, and there is some evidence that this decorative plaster was picked out in colour.

This lighter timber construction was often used for the smaller, poorer-class houses, but it is sometimes found in quite large houses in areas where no other suitable local materials were available. Large scale use of timber for shipbuilding at this period meant that it was having to be used more sparingly in houses. Light timber-framed construction continued into the nineteenth century in some areas, the walls being covered externally with plaster, tile-hanging or weatherboarding.

The earlier timber-framed buildings had the panels filled with wattle and daub. Chestnut or hazel rods were inserted into grooves in the horizontal members, and willow or hazel withies were woven round these,

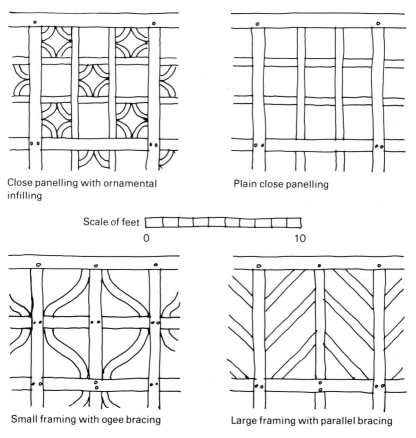

Close panelling with ornamental infilling

Plain close panelling

Scale of feet

0   10

Small framing with ogee bracing

Large framing with parallel bracing

All these forms were used in the sixteenth and seventeenth centuries, in better class buildings - mainly in the North and West. Like close studding, they used a considerable amount of timber and were therefore expensive. The intermediate members were decorative only.

Fig. 39 **Timber-framing, typical ornamental forms.**

basket fashion, the whole being covered with a daub of clay, chalk and mud. This was finished with lime plaster and limewash. In the South and East this limewash was sometimes continued over the timbers, and it might be tinted with ochre or umber. Where this was not done, the timbers were generally left unstained. In the North and West there is some evidence that the timbers were coloured, particularly in later buildings, with ornamental patterned framing. The general habit of blackening all timbers was a nineteenth century development.

By the sixteenth century in the South and East, and rather later in other areas, this wattle and daub filling was beginning to be replaced by brick.

141

Sometimes this brickwork is original, sometimes a replacement of wattle and daub. Early bricks were generally longer, thinner and more irregular than modern ones, and early brick filling was sometimes laid to a herring-bone pattern.

Mention has been made earlier of jettying in timber-framed buildings: the construction of upper floors to overhang those below. This first appears in the fifteenth century Wealden houses. By the mid sixteenth century it was becoming less common, and in rural areas it is comparatively rare after the end of the century, particularly in the South-east. In other areas, especially in towns, this form of construction continued into the early seventeenth century.

One problem in dating and analysing timber-framed houses is the ease with which timbers can be moved and re-used. This is often indicated by the presence of mortice holes and notches for which there appears to be no logical reason, another source of the popular view that houses were sometimes built with 'old ships' timbers'. It may well be that such timbers were used near seaports where ships were broken up, or in coastal areas noted for wrecking. Further inland, however, it is unlikely that much timber was transported long distances over medieval and Tudor roads, when equally good timber was probably available near at hand. Timbers were often re-used from other demolished or altered buildings, as the cost of materials was high relative to that of labour. Apart from this utilitarian re-use, timber-framed buildings are perhaps subject more than any others to deliberate faking to create an 'olde worlde' effect. Close examination may reveal that some venerable-looking timbers have no structural function, and may not even be framed into the original work.

Cob

Cob, a primitive form of concrete made of chalk, mud and straw, was used from medieval times, particularly in areas lacking a good supply of suitable timber for building. Later, as other materials became available, cob tended to be used mainly for smaller houses and cottages. The materials and methods used varied in different localities. The best and most durable cob contained a high proportion of chalk, so that most of the earlier surviving cob houses are found in the chalk downland areas. Cob was used until the nineteenth century, but by this time it was often faced with brick, or mathematical tiles.

The older cob houses were usually plastered and limewashed, and were built off a base of stone, flint or brick. Evidence that a house is built of cob

A late medieval yeoman's house at Larkfield, Kent. The timbers have been limewashed with the panels in traditional style.

may be found in the thickness of the walls, often built to a batter, that is, tapering from maximum thickness at the base. External angles are sometimes slightly rounded.

Dating of cob is not easy and is best considered in relation to the size, plan and general quality of the house. The materials used for the wall base may provide a clue: in the older houses this will be of stone or flint; a brick base suggests a later date, depending upon when brick was first used in the area, particularly in smaller houses.

As an alternative to cob, chalk blocks were sometimes used for walling, probably from medieval times. These walls were normally plastered and are only discovered during alterations or demolition. Another variation, clay lump, was used in certain areas such as East Anglia and Cambridgeshire. This is really a form of unbaked brick, and like chalk block it was normally plastered, and is difficult to date, except in relation to other features of the building.

143

Historical survey of a house: The exterior

Stone

Except in areas where rubble stone was easily available, from shallow quarries near at hand or from demolished buildings, stone was not often used for small houses before the sixteenth or early seventeenth centuries. The earliest surviving stone houses, those of medieval date, are likely to have been built as manor houses, merchants' houses in towns, or occasionally as hunting lodges.

By the seventeenth century, good quality small stone houses were being built in the limestone areas, such as the Cotswolds, where there was now a tradition of good masonry construction. Such houses were rarer in the poorer areas of the North until the mid seventeenth century. Even by this time, stone was only used for smaller and medium sized houses in areas which were reasonably accessible from the quarries.

Ashlar stone (stone cut into rectangular blocks and laid with fine mortar joints) was more expensive than rubble (stones of irregular size and shape, laid with thicker joints) and its use generally indicates a better-class building.

Stone was often used in conjunction with brickwork for quoins, door and window surrounds, and other decorative features, particularly in houses of more formal design. In the late eighteenth century an artificial stone, known as Coade Stone, was introduced and was in use until the 1830s. This material enabled decorative features to be mass-produced, foreshadowing modern developments in this field. A cheaper alternative, popular in the nineteenth century, was to form these features in plaster or cement, sometimes painted in imitation of stone.

From the Middle Ages until the eighteenth century it was common for rubble walling to be limewashed externally, and even ashlar was sometimes treated in this way. The White Tower at the Tower of London is believed to have been named from its appearance resulting from regular lime-washing. The limewash, particularly when mixed with tallow, helped to improve the weather-resistance of porous stone, and the fact that the wash was often tinted with umber or ochre suggests that the treatment also had a decorative purpose.

In the nineteenth century, when bare stone became fashionable, many old stone houses had their limewash removed. Generally, only the smaller and humbler houses, and those in remote rural areas, escaped this treatment.

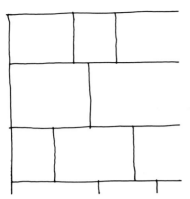

Fine ashlar

The stone is accurately squared and laid with very fine joints. Generally found in the best quality work.

Rough ashlar

The stone is roughly squared and laid with wider joints. Less expensive than fine ashlar.

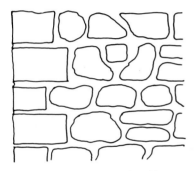

Coursed rubble with rough ashlar quoins

Irregular-shaped stones laid in horizontal courses.

Random rubble with brick quoins

Irregular-shaped stones not laid in courses. Mortar joints are relatively wide.

Fig. 40 **Typical stone walling patterns. All these forms of walling were used in most periods. Generally, ashlar was used in better-class work, and rubble in cheaper work, but this was not invariable. Differences of walling in the same building may indicate work of different dates. On the other hand, ashlar may be found in the more important and rubble in the less important facades.**

Flint

This material, like stone, was generally used in areas where it was easily available, particularly in the chalk downlands. Because of the difficulty of constructing good vertical angles in flint, it was often combined with other materials for the quoins of the building, and for door and window

145

Historical survey of a house:

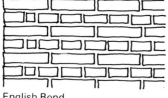

English Bond

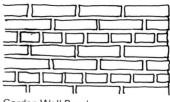

Garden Wall Bond

Both these bonds were in use until the end of the seventeenth century. The earlier, thinner bricks are shown here but bricks of modern size were in use by the mid-seventeenth century.

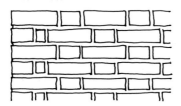

Flemish Bond

This was usual from the late seventeenth century. The darker, more burnt 'headers' were sometimes used decoratively.

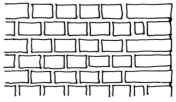

Header Bond

This was popular in some areas in the eighteenth century. It was often used with contrasting coloured bricks at quoins and jambs.

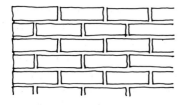

Stretcher Bond

Only used for walls 4½ inches thick. It generally indicates modern cavity walling.

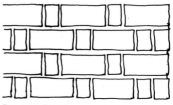

Rat-trap Bond

Bricks were laid on edge. Found in cheaper work in the nineteenth and twentieth centuries.

Fig. 41 **Brickwork, various bonds.**

146

surrounds. In earlier examples, flint was generally combined with stone in this way, but by the seventeenth century brick was being used. Sometimes flint and brick or stone were used in alternate bands, partly to strengthen the wall and partly for decoration.

In East Anglia the flints on better-class buildings were sometimes knapped and cut to a square shape. This knapped flintwork might be combined with stone to form ornamental patterns, but this was more common in churches and larger houses than in the smaller houses.

Brick

After the cessation of Roman building, brick was not reintroduced into England until the Middle Ages, but not before the fifteenth century was it used in smaller houses. It appeared first in the South and East, spreading across the country and gradually replacing timber-framing and cob for the better-class houses. There are few small brick houses dating from before the early seventeenth century, but brick was being used for chimney stacks, particularly in timber-framed houses, by the sixteenth century, when many early open halls were being floored over.

By the late seventeenth century smaller brick houses were quite common, and by the eighteenth century brick had become the most usual material for these houses. Many timber and cob houses were refaced in brick at this period.

The earliest (post-Roman) bricks were rather longer, thinner and more irregular in shape than modern bricks. By the mid seventeenth century bricks were being made of a size nearer those of today, although there was still some variation. An Act of Parliament of 1776 fixed the size of bricks to be used throughout the country at $8\frac{1}{2}$ by 4 by $2\frac{1}{2}$ inches. After 1784, when the first brick tax was introduced, larger bricks were made, since the tax was calculated on the number of individual bricks used and not on the volume of brickwork. Some bricks at this period were as large as 10 by 5 by 3 inches. In 1803 a further tax was levied on these large bricks, and this was avoided by reducing their size to 9 by $4\frac{1}{2}$ by 3 inches. The brick tax was removed in 1850, and since then the size of the brick has been largely standardized, brickwork rising four courses to a foot. In the north of England, however, larger bricks, rising four courses to thirteen inches, were in use for much of the nineteenth century.

In early brick buildings the bonding is often irregular, but English Bond became usual by the end of the sixteenth century. Flemish Bond was introduced in the seventeenth century, and had largely replaced English

Bond by the early eighteenth century. In some places Header Bond was popular in the eighteenth century, and the dark headers resulting from the clamp method of burning or firing were used to form ornamental patterns.

In the sixteenth, seventeenth and early eighteenth centuries red brick was popular. By the eighteenth century grey and brown bricks were being used, generally with red bricks as dressings to door and window openings and as quoins at the external angles. Later in the eighteenth century red brick was less favoured in better-class houses, particularly in London, as it was considered too bright for current taste. Brown and grey bricks were now more popular, and in London the familiar yellow Stock became almost universal. By the second half of the nineteenth century, however, this London Stock had, like Welsh slate, begun to acquire a working-class image, and red bricks came back into favour for better-class houses.

By the nineteenth century machine-made bricks were appearing, and these eventually replaced hand-made bricks except for the best quality work. These machine-made bricks are generally smoother and more regular in appearance than the older bricks.

Roofs

Having studied the walling materials, let us look at the roof. One problem concerning dating is that roofs need renewal more often than walls. A tiled or slated roof probably needs stripping and re-laying about every hundred years, and thatch has an even shorter life. Roofs are therefore more likely than walls to be replaced with more modern or cheaper materials as these become available. When we look at a roof we have to try to decide not only how long it has been there, but whether it is a replacement, later in date than the main building.

From medieval times until the late fifteenth century most small houses were roofed with thatch or, where oak was available, with shingles (thin slabs of oak, laid in a similar way to tiles). It is almost impossible to date a thatched roof, since the thatch is unlikely to be more than sixty years old at the most. Where an original thatched roof has been replaced with tiles or slates, evidence of the earlier finish may sometimes be seen in the weatherings — projecting courses of stone or brick well above the later roof line, on chimney stacks and adjoining walls or parapets.

Tiles, like bricks, first appeared in the South-east and were being used on the Wealden yeomen's houses by about 1500. They were not common on small houses in the North and West until the later seventeenth century. The older tiles are generally more irregular in shape than modern ones, and often have a definite 'camber' or curve in their profile. They do not normally have nibs, like modern tiles, and they were fixed with wood pegs. Sometimes they were bedded on hay or straw for insulation, and to prevent the entry of driving rain or snow. This of course can only be seen from the interior of the roof. Lead flashings and weatherings to tile and slate roofs only became common in the eighteenth and nineteenth centuries.

Pantiles seem to have been used first in East Anglia, probably due to Flemish influence, in the seventeenth century. By the eighteenth century they were being used over much of the eastern half of the country. In the West they are rarely found on houses but common on farm buildings.

In areas where suitable stone was available, stone slates were used on better-class buildings from medieval times, but were probably rare on smaller houses until the seventeenth century. They were fixed with wood pegs or, occasionally, sheep's bones. They were normally laid in diminishing courses, with the smaller slates used higher up the roof slope. This may have been partly for aesthetic reasons, as well as to make use of the heavier slates near the bottom of the rafters. It also reduced the number of joints in the slating in the area where the flow of water was greatest.

True slates were used in areas where they were quarried — Cornwall, Wales and the Lake District — at the same period. With the introduction of cheap transport, particularly after the development of the railways, Welsh slate was widely used, first for better-class buildings and, by the mid nineteenth century, for artisan housing. This gave slate a working-class image, and probably accounted for its unpopularity in the present century, the result of which is that many slate quarries now lie derelict.

Apart from the materials used, the form of the roof can sometimes indicate its age. As a rough guide it is fair to say that the older the roof, the steeper its pitch is likely to be. The older traditional materials needed a steep pitch to throw off rain and snow, and as the old houses were generally only one room deep this presented few problems. Later materials, pantiles and Welsh slate, as well as some forms of stone slating, could be laid to a flatter pitch.

The earliest roofs on small houses had plain overhanging eaves without gutters or downpipes. This is still normal practice with thatch. When gutters and downpipes first appeared they were generally of lead, or of timber lined with lead for the gutters. Some of the early lead rainwater heads were quite ornamental and they are often dated, but it must be remembered that this date applies only to the rainwater head, and not necessarily to the building, which may be earlier.

Historical survey of a house: The exterior

Cast iron was introduced for gutters and downpipes in the nineteenth century. At first these copied the designs used in lead, including square-section downpipes. While these were generally satisfactory for lead, they were not very practicable in cast iron, particularly when they were fixed close to the wall and could not be painted at the back. As a result, they tended to rust and split, causing dampness in the walls. Circular-section downpipes, less attractive to look at, were more practical in cast iron.

By the late seventeenth century it became fashionable to hide the exposed feet of the rafters at the eaves with a moulded timber cornice. In London this was one of the features prohibited by the Building Act of 1707, which required the roof to be finished behind a brick or stone parapet to help prevent spread of fire. In central London this provides a useful guide to dating, although the Act does not seem to have been immediately obeyed in all parts of London. Eventually this feature was copied elsewhere, first in towns and later in rural areas, although it was never universal in small houses. By the late eighteenth century, however, the roof was becoming less important architecturally, and with the introduction of Welsh slate, permitting the roof to be of flatter pitch, it was sometimes almost completely concealed behind the parapet. Flat lead roofs, being more expensive than low pitched slate roofs, were less often found on smaller houses.

After noting the general form of the house and the materials of the walls and the roof, we should now look at the architectural features, doors, windows and chimneys.

Doors

In late medieval and early Tudor houses the doors were either hung directly to the walls, or on heavy-section timber frames, often with arched heads. Modern-type hinges were not used, the strap hinges being hung on iron pins or 'rides'. In fourteenth and early fifteenth century work the two-centred arch was common. By the late fifteenth century the four-centred arch had appeared, and this continued in some areas well into the seventeenth century in a modified form, becoming more and more flattened in outline. Occasionally the ogee or double curved arch was used, as was the 'shouldered' arch, the last being typical of the late fifteenth and sixteenth centuries. By the end of the seventeenth century the plain square frame was most common, and in the smallest and plainest houses this form

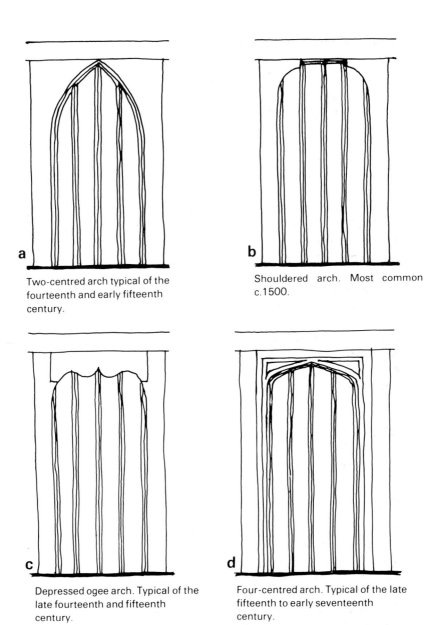

a — Two-centred arch typical of the fourteenth and early fifteenth century.

b — Shouldered arch. Most common c.1500.

c — Depressed ogee arch. Typical of the late fourteenth and fifteenth century.

d — Four-centred arch. Typical of the late fifteenth to early seventeenth century.

Scale of feet

0   5

Fig. 42 **Doors and door frames, early types. These are all shown in timber, but are also found in stone, particularly in better-class houses.**

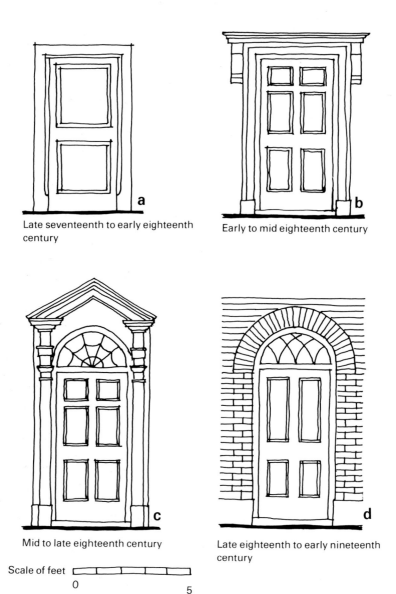

Late seventeenth to early eighteenth century

Early to mid eighteenth century

Mid to late eighteenth century

Late eighteenth to early nineteenth century

Scale of feet

0   5

Fig. 43 **Doors and doorcases, typical later forms.**

is found from earliest times. In better-class work the door frames were often moulded.

The doors at this period were constructed of vertical planks, strengthened with horizontal rails on the inner face. The joints between the planks

152

might be rebated, or covered with moulded fillets, and sometimes the planks themselves were moulded or shaped in section.

By the end of the seventeenth century the influence of the Renaissance was affecting door design. The frames were less massive and the doors were hung on hinges more like those of today. In the smaller and simpler houses vertical planked doors were still common though they were now often of softwood rather than of oak. In the houses of more sophisticated design panelled doors were often used, with four or six panels, often moulded and sometimes with raised panels.

The treatment of the head of an external door opening can also help us in dating. In the earlier periods porches were rare in smaller houses, but the doorway might be protected by a lean-to or 'pentice' roof on brackets. By the late seventeenth or early eighteenth century this feature had evolved into a flat classical door hood, supported on console brackets, sometimes quite elaborately moulded or carved. In the later eighteenth century a classical pediment, straight-sided or segmental, was popular and the door frame was often flanked by moulded pilasters forming a complete frame to the doorway (fig. 43c).

In London successive Building Acts discouraged the use of projecting timberwork on facades, and after the Act of 1774 it tended to disappear, door openings being emphasized only by a more ornamental treatment of the surrounding brick or stonework. As with roof finishes this change gradually affected much building outside London.

Porches were originally functional, protecting the door from the weather and making the house more draughtproof. As with so many features, the opportunity was taken to introduce decorative elements reflecting the current architectural fashion. By the end of the eighteenth century open porches of ornamental cast iron were popular, their functional origins apparently forgotten. These trellis-type porches and verandas were often added to older houses at this time.

Windows

In the late medieval and early Tudor periods windows in smaller houses were generally unglazed and fitted with internal shutters. Only the wealthy could afford window glass. Occasionally in the better-class houses windows of traditional Gothic form, with arched stone heads, are found, similar to those in medieval churches, but normally the windows in smaller houses were square-headed and divided into lights by stone or, more often, timber uprights or mullions, square in section and set diagonally. This form of

Historical survey of a house:

The original unglazed window in the hall of a small Wealden house: Prings Cottage, Halling, Kent.

window survived into the seventeenth century for less important rooms such as pantries and dairies (fig. 44a).

By the mid sixteenth century window glass was within the means of the builders of medium sized and smaller houses, and the design of the early mullioned windows was modified to take glazing. This was in leaded panes, rectangular or diamond shaped, with iron opening lights. The mullions themselves were modified. In better-class houses and in areas where stone was easily obtained, the mullions were usually of stone. In smaller houses and in all timber-framed buildings the windows were still of timber, the mullions being similar to those of stone, but generally lighter in section (fig. 44b).

The earliest glazed windows had mullions with straight splays, but these were soon superseded by those having a slightly hollowed splay, giving a rather lighter effect. This detail was typical of the late sixteenth century and the early seventeenth century. Later in the seventeenth century this section had given place to one with a convex moulding, with square fillets at the angles (fig. 45). In some areas, however, the hollow splay was revived in the late seventeenth century, but by this period a plain square section mullion was more common, and continued in use into the eighteenth century in some places.

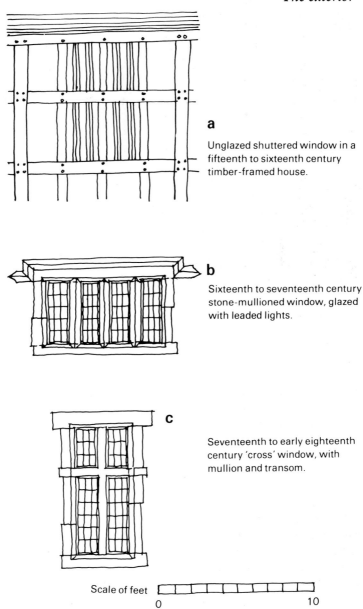

a

Unglazed shuttered window in a fifteenth to sixteenth century timber-framed house.

b

Sixteenth to seventeenth century stone-mullioned window, glazed with leaded lights.

c

Seventeenth to early eighteenth century 'cross' window, with mullion and transom.

Scale of feet

0   10

Fig. 44 **Evolution of the mullioned window. Both later forms are also found with timber mullions, generally lighter in section than stone.**

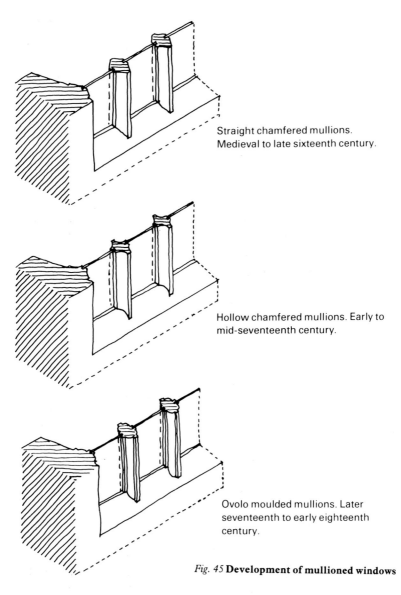

Straight chamfered mullions.
Medieval to late sixteenth century.

Hollow chamfered mullions. Early to
mid-seventeenth century.

Ovolo moulded mullions. Later
seventeenth to early eighteenth
century.

Fig. 45 **Development of mullioned windows**

In the sixteenth and seventeenth centuries the windows were normally finished with separate hood moulds or weather moulds above the window heads. This feature, originally intended to protect the window from rainwater running down the wall face, was also treated as a decorative feature. By the late seventeenth century these separate hood moulds were often superseded by a continuous moulding over all the adjoining windows, and this feature developed into the fully continuous string course, or band course, marking the storey heights. In the eighteenth century, in brick buildings, the last vestiges of this feature may be seen in the projecting band of three or four courses of brickwork at the various upper floor levels.

The proportions of the early windows were generally rather long and low, with a horizontal emphasis. By the mid seventeenth century this proportion was changing, particularly in the larger houses and those showing the influence of the Renaissance; the windows were becoming taller and narrower, probably echoing the increased ceiling heights now becoming popular. The windows of this type were often only two lights in width, and as well as a vertical mullion they had a horizontal member, a transom, forming a cross in the window opening (fig. 44c). In the smaller houses and cottages, less affected by changes in fashion and retaining lower ceiling heights, this change of proportion was less marked.

By the eighteenth century the mullioned and transomed window with its leaded lights and iron casements had, except in some rural areas, given way to the double-hung timber sash window, divided into small panes by glazing bars, so typical of the Georgian style. In early sash windows the frames were flush with the outer face of the wall, and the glazing bars were quite heavy in section, the mouldings being a smaller version of the convex moulded mullions of the previous century (fig. 46a). The London Building Acts of 1707 and 1709 required the sashes to be set back four inches from the wall face, and this change later affected other parts of the country. Another change may be seen in the design of the glazing bars, which became progressively lighter in section, and very slender indeed by the early nineteenth century.

In the seventeenth and early eighteenth centuries window surrounds in brick houses were often enriched and emphasized with contrasting brick dressings, and their arches were given projecting, sometimes carved, keystones. Later in the century these features were less common, reflecting the general trend of simpler facade designs.

The London Building Act of 1774 required the window frames not only to be set back from the wall face but to be recessed behind reveals, so that little of the frame was visible externally (fig. 46c). As with the earlier changes in London, this fashion was eventually adopted in other areas.

By the late eighteenth century other glazing patterns had appeared. Glazing bars might be arranged in a Gothic pattern. In the early nineteenth century one popular design had fairly large panes in the centre of each

157

sash, with a border of narrower panes (fig. 46d). By the mid nineteenth century, as plate glass became available, glazing bars were omitted and the sashes were glazed in a single sheet. At this time, too, many earlier windows had their glazing bars removed, rather spoiling the appearance of the building.

In the smaller houses and cottages the old mullioned windows were often replaced in the eighteenth century by side-hung timber casements, or by horizontally sliding sashes, both of which were cheaper to construct than the double-hung sashes, and which suited the more horizontal proportions of the windows in these houses. Some earlier windows actually had their mullions cut out to accommodate timber sashes. In other cases timber sashes were fitted between the mullions, replacing the lead lights and iron frames.

When blocked windows are found in old houses it is often assumed that this was done during the period when the Window Tax was in force, from 1695 to the end of the eighteenth century. This is certainly true in some cases, but it is not the only explanation. Sometimes a blocked window indicates an internal replanning whereby the window has become redundant. This can only be checked by an internal inspection. In the eighteenth century, when a symmetrical facade was considered essential, false or 'blind' windows were sometimes inserted to balance actual windows. In these the infilling would be recessed, but it was generally bonded into the surrounding walling, unlike most later fillings. Sometimes the blind windows were painted to simulate actual windows.

An alternative to timber casements quite common in the early nineteenth century was the cast iron casement, divided into small panes, not unlike lead lights in appearance. Cast iron was also much used at this time for ornamental balconies to upper windows, particularly in better-class houses and in towns. Various standard designs were produced for these, the anthemion (or honeysuckle) being a popular motif.

Chimney stacks

As we have seen, chimney stacks first appeared in the medium sized and smaller houses in the mid sixteenth century, both as features of new buildings and introduced into older ones, often in conjunction with the flooring-over of an open hall. Both stone and brick were used from the start and, less often, cob, sometimes for the lower part of the stack below the roof and, occasionally, for the whole structure. In some early examples, particularly in timber-framed houses, stacks on the end gable walls were

Typical early eighteenth century window frame flush with the wall face. Heavy section glazing bars.

Typical mid eighteenth century window frame set back from wall face. Slightly more slender glazing bars.

Typical late eighteenth century window. Frame set back from wall face and recessed behind reveals. Very slender glazing bars.

Early nineteenth century window with 'bordered' sashes. Later in the century glazing bars were often omitted completely.

Scale of feet

0   5

Fig. 46 **Eighteenth and nineteenth century windows**

built projecting from the outer face of the wall. Later, they were usually incorporated in the wall itself. Sometimes brick was used for a chimney inserted in the gable wall of a stone building, and this shows up plainly in the external wall.

Because of their exposure to the weather chimneys built of a soft stone often deteriorated more quickly than the main walling, and they were sometimes rebuilt in brick.

The earliest stacks were quite massive and rather plain in design, but their potential decorative value was soon discovered. In the late sixteenth and seventeenth centuries, in all but the simplest houses, brick stacks were often elaborately decorated using specially moulded bricks. By the later seventeenth and eighteenth centuries the influence of the Renaissance may be seen in the classical capping mouldings given to stacks, particularly those of ashlar stone. Chimney pots were rare on smaller houses until the nineteenth century, when they were often added to older stacks to improve the draught of the flues, particularly as a result of the more widespread use of coal as a fuel rather than wood.

The positions of the chimney stacks as seen from the exterior can often tell us something about the basic plan of the house. A stack just to one side of the main entrance suggests a three-room plan with a stack backing on to the through-passage. One immediately above the main entrance suggests a lobby entrance plan, and stacks on the end gables suggest the symmetrical plan of the late seventeenth and eighteenth centuries.

In the case of a town house the external inspection may not be as straightforward as that of a detached country house. The town house may well be in a terrace, and the rear may not be easily accessible. If, however, it is possible to see the back of the house, perhaps from a rear street or passageway, this may well reveal that the house is much older than at first appears. Town houses, certainly those which have been used as shops or for other commercial purposes, are likely to have had their main facades altered, or even completely rebuilt. The insertion of a modern shop front, combined with a remodelling of much of the ground floor, can give a completely false impression of the true age of a house.

With medieval town houses on their typical long narrow plots, the rear garden may have been built over, and the back of the original house therefore becomes very difficult to examine and interpret. In these cases an aerial photograph or the view from a church tower or other high building can be invaluable.

8
Historical survey of a house. The interior

Having noted all we can about the exterior of our house, let us go inside. If we are going to make a serious study of the house we must carry out a measured survey. Instructions for this are given in Appendix I. From the completed survey drawing we should be able to pick out the original form of the house from the successive alterations and additions. These are often indicated by such things as changes in wall thicknesses and directions, and changes in floor levels.

Before starting the measured survey, however, it is best to look all over the house and note the features which may help in dating it. The most important of these are the plan form and the roof structure.

The external inspection may have shown us whether the house is, or was originally, of single or double-pile form (i.e. one room or two rooms deep), and the internal inspection may verify this. If, for instance, the central spine wall of a double-pile house, running parallel to the front and back walls, is unusually thick, and if it shows signs of blocked door and window openings, it may once have been the external rear wall. Old houses were often 'doubled up' in the eighteenth and nineteenth centuries.

If the roof space is accessible this should be thoroughly inspected. Unless it has been completely renewed, the roof can tell us a great deal about the house. The materials used should be noted. Oak was the usual material until the late seventeenth century. Other native hardwoods, such as chestnut and elm, were sometimes used but pine and other imported softwoods were more usual from the late seventeenth century onwards. Generally, the heavier the timbers the older the roof is likely to be. Again, until the late seventeenth century, the common rafters were either approximately square in section, or were wider than their depth. After this period they were made deeper and narrower.

Examination of the roof can often indicate whether the house was originally of open hall form. Signs of smoke-blackening on the timbers are a definite confirmation of this. Sometimes this may be difficult to distinguish from dirt, or a later preservative treatment, but it may be possible to tell whether the roof was originally designed to be seen. The angles of the main beams may be chamfered or moulded. Wind-bracing had some functional value, but it was also an ornamental feature, and if it is arranged in a definite pattern it may well be that it was intended to be seen. A 'visible' roof with no signs of smoke-blackening may indicate an open hall with a wall fireplace, or even a first-floor hall.

In some houses originally built with open halls remains of the original ceilings have survived. These were of wattle, laid over the rafters to form a foundation for the thatch. Occasionally the common rafters were omitted, the wattling being laid directly over the purlins.

Until the late seventeenth century, and later in some areas, it was usual for the roof trusses to be made at the carpenter's yard, framed together to make sure that they fitted, taken to pieces for transport to the building, and re-assembled there. To make sure that the correct sections were fitted together at the site each truss member was numbered, using Roman numerals. If these can be found they may indicate whether the building has been lengthened or shortened, or if the roof has been reconstructed, since when this happened the trusses were not always put back in their original order.

The actual design of the roof will also help us in dating it. In many Wealden houses the original crown posts with their curved braces survive, hidden in an attic or roof space. These roofs date from the late fourteenth to the mid sixteenth century. Generally the earlier crown posts are short and thick, the later ones taller and more slender. The earlier ones usually had four-way bracing, to the struts and the collar purlin. In some of the later roofs the crown post was braced two ways, to the collar purlin only. These crown post roofs ceased to be constructed after open halls were superseded. Often, when an old open hall was floored over, the tie-beam was in an inconvenient position about three feet above the new floor level. It was sometimes cut away to take a door opening in a partition, or even removed entirely and replaced by a collar beam at a higher level.

Roofs of cruck construction can also be identified quite easily. Surviving true cruck roofs may date from the late fifteenth or early sixteenth century; jointed cruck roofs are generally rather later, from the sixteenth or seventeenth centuries. After this period, roofs in smaller houses were usually quite plain in design, with tie-beam trusses supporting purlins, and common rafters over narrower spans. King-post and queen-post trusses are found over wider double-pile spans.

The trusses should also be examined to see which, if any, were once

A jointed cruck truss in a former open-hall house, visible on the landing.

filled with partitions. This is particularly important in open hall houses, and it can help us to work out the original plan form. If the partitions themselves have gone, their positions may be traced by holes in the roof timbers to take studs, i.e. the uprights of a wattle and daub partition. Another feature to note is the relationship of the roof trusses to the chimney stacks, which may show whether the stacks were built at the same time as the roof, or whether they are later insertions. When a house was enlarged by building new wings, this is often apparent in the roof construction.

Apart from the general plan form and the roof structure, the following features will help us in dating and working out the history of the house.

Chimneys

We have seen how the position of chimneys can help us in working out the original plan form, and thus with the dating of the house. Their size, only visible inside the house, is also helpful. The early chimneys were very large, as were the fireplace openings where large logs of timber were burnt on 'dogs' or, rather later, in basket grates. By the late seventeenth century smaller grates were used as coal became more generally available. The fireplace openings were now smaller, as were the chimney stacks themselves. In many houses large old fireplace openings were reduced in size to take later forms of grate, perhaps in conjunction with a general refurbishing of the room in Georgian style. In these cases, the overall size

163

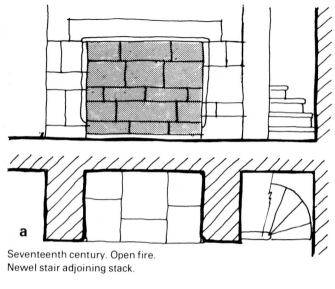

Seventeenth century. Open fire.
Newel stair adjoining stack.

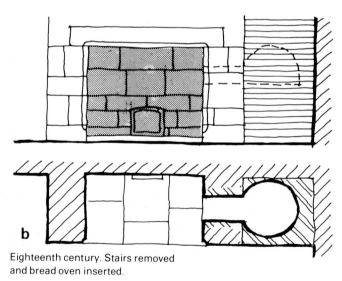

Eighteenth century. Stairs removed
and bread oven inserted.

Scale of feet

0   5   10

Fig. 47 **The farmhouse hall or kitchen fireplace**

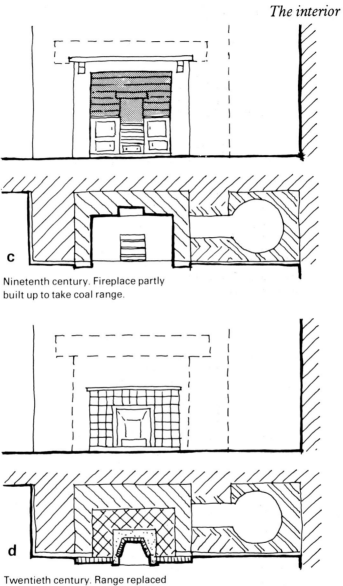

c Ninetenth century. Fireplace partly
built up to take coal range.

d Twentieth century. Range replaced
by open fireplace.

Scale of feet

0   5   10

Historical survey of a house:

A modern fireplace in an old house often conceals a larger, earlier opening.

of the chimney stack may indicate that it is much earlier than is suggested by the present fireplace opening (fig. 47).

The large early fireplace openings had stone or timber lintels, sometimes moulded and shaped into a very flattened version of the four-centred or Tudor arch. The later, smaller, openings were spanned by brick arches, and by the nineteenth century these were often supported on iron chimney bars (fig. 48).

In many old houses brick bread ovens have been incorporated in the hall or kitchen fireplace. Most of these date from the eighteenth and early nineteenth centuries and were often inserted into older fireplaces, as may be indicated by a change in the brickwork. Occasionally a circular curing chamber for bacon may be found on one side of the fireplace, sometimes wrongly identified as a 'priest's hole'.

Twelfth to fourteenth century.
Projecting hood carried on piers.
Generally of stone. Timber and
plaster sometimes used.

Fifteenth to seventeenth century.
Moulded stone surround with four-
centred arch. Also found in timber.
Iron dogs supported logs, providing
improved draught.

Late seventeenth to early
eighteenth century. Opening
surrounded by a bold bolection
mould. Sometimes finished with a
cornice. Fire carried in an iron
basket.

Late eighteenth to early nineteenth
century. Fire surround of classical
design, with more refined
mouldings. Hob grate designed for
coal-burning.

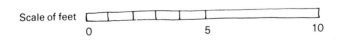

Scale of feet

0   5   10

Fig. 48 **Development of the fireplace**

Historical survey of a house:

Former doors, windows and partitions

Evidence may sometimes be found inside the house, indicated by cracks in the plaster, recesses in the walls, and mortice holes, grooves and slots in the undersides of beams. More often they may be revealed during alterations, and they should always be recorded and marked on the survey plan. Sometimes a whole window, complete with leaded glazing, is found buried under plaster.

Floor levels and materials

In the smaller houses the earliest ground floors were either of beaten earth, stone flags or lime ash (a form of hard plaster), depending on the class and quality of the building. By the seventeenth century brick and tile floors were becoming more common, particularly where stone was not easily available. The early tiles were unglazed and larger than modern tiles. By the eighteenth century timber floors were introduced, and in the nineteenth century they were usual for living rooms, stone or tiles being retained for kitchens and service rooms.

Changes in floor levels should be noted, especially if these appear original. In long-houses, the byre beyond the through-passage was often at a lower level to facilitate drainage, and this feature sometimes survived the conversion of the byre into a kitchen. Conversely, the floor of the pantry was sometimes raised a step higher than that of the hall. Sometimes, in small houses, this was the only distinction between the two areas.

Upper floors were usually of timber, although occasionally a hard plaster was used. Before the eighteenth century floor boards were often wider than modern ones and were generally of hardwood, elm being particularly popular. Unexplained changes of level in upper floors may indicate either that the house is of more than one build, or that part of it was an open hall.

Doors

The evolution of the external door has been described in the last chapter, and internal doors were of similar design but generally rather lighter in construction. Since internal doors are quite easily replaced, we shall often find eighteenth-century panelled doors in earlier buildings. Sometimes the old frames were retained as their removal created more disturbance to the structure, and a sixteenth or early seventeenth century heavy oak frame may be found half concealed by an eighteenth century architrave.

Windows

The development of window design has been traced in the previous chapter, but their internal details are worth studying. It is sometimes possible to see whether a window opening has been increased or reduced in size, and cupboards and recesses in external or internal walls may prove to be former window openings, sometimes retaining their mullions and surrounds.

As previously indicated, the earliest windows were unglazed, often with horizontally sliding shutters. Sometimes the grooves for these may be seen in the head and cill of a window later adapted to take glazing. Alternatively, hinged wooden shutters were sometimes used, secured when shut by an iron bar, and even if the shutters themselves have gone the slot or staple for the bar may be seen in the jambs or mullions.

When glazed windows became more common shutters were still used both to conserve heat and to keep out intruders. The early examples were generally of oak and quite plain, but by the eighteenth century panelled shutters became common, folding back into the window jambs. Sometimes these have been fixed back open, and only the surviving hinges (generally painted over) distinguish them from panelled jamb linings. In the late eighteenth and early nineteenth centuries vertical sliding shutters are sometimes found, rising on sash cords with counterbalanced weights similar to, and inside, the sash window itself.

Where early wrought-iron opening casements have survived, they may retain their original fasteners and stays. These were generally made by a local blacksmith, and several examples of similar design may be found in a particular area. In timber-mullioned windows the iron casements were sometimes hinged in the normal modern way, but often they were hung on iron pins or rides in the frame similarly to those in stone windows. In the earliest double-hung sash windows the lower sash was often fixed, and even the upper sash was not always hung on cords and weights. Wooden stops were formed in the frame to prevent the sash opening beyond a certain point. By the mid eighteenth century it was usual for both sashes to be openable, with cords and lead weights.

Partitions

In the fifteenth, sixteenth and early seventeenth centuries internal partitions, as distinct from loadbearing walls, were of two main types. The first type was timber-framed, with wattle and daub filling, similar to the

Historical survey of a house:

Fig. 49
Plank and muntin partitions

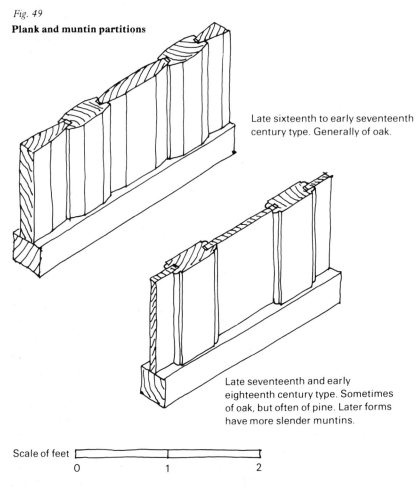

Late sixteenth to early seventeenth century type. Generally of oak.

Late seventeenth and early eighteenth century type. Sometimes of oak, but often of pine. Later forms have more slender muntins.

Scale of feet

0   1   2

external walls of timber-framed houses. The second type was entirely of timber, consisting of timber uprights, or 'muntins', grooved down their edges, into which thinner timber planks were slotted. The muntins were framed into horizontal members at the top and bottom, the head and the cill. In very plain work the muntins might be left simply squared, but the faces were more often chamfered to give a lighter effect, and in the more important rooms they were often moulded (fig. 49).

Until the later seventeenth century these plank and muntin partitions were generally of oak, but later painted softwood was used. In cottages this form of partition continued in use into the nineteenth century, the muntins becoming very light in section: but in better-class houses it was superseded by the stud partition, plastered over the studs. By the eighteenth century plaster was usually applied on rent or split laths, but rushes were used as lathing in many areas into the nineteenth century. Sawn laths took the place of rent laths in the later nineteenth century.

Panelling

Panelling was introduced in the Middle Ages, but was not usual in smaller houses until the Tudor period. Originally it was intended to make the rooms warmer and drier, but as with many utilitarian features its decorative possibilities were soon recognised.

The earliest panelling was of oak or other native hardwood and was framed up in fairly small panels. The main horizontal and vertical framing members were generally moulded, the earliest form of this being a series of scribed grooves on the edges of the framing members (fig. 50a). When fully developed mouldings appeared they were at first worked on the solid members to produce a 'mason's mitre', with the joint between the horizontal and vertical members coinciding with the outer line of the moulding (fig. 50b). Later in the Tudor period the horizontal member was cut away to allow a true 'carpenter's mitre' to be formed in the moulding, with the joint between the horizontal and vertical members coinciding with the inner line of the moulding (fig. 50c).

Sometimes the panels themselves were left plain, but often in better-class work they were 'raised' so that the centre of the panel was in line with the face of the framing members, and was worked back to fit into the grooves in their edges. This meant that the panel was worked out of a thicker piece of oak, and this shaping brought out the grain of the timber. This raised panelling developed into the 'linenfold' panel design typical of the later Tudor and early Stuart periods (fig. 50d).

In prestigious houses in the seventeenth century, the panels were increased in size and classical mouldings were introduced. The whole room was now treated as an architectural composition comprising the skirting, dado, upper wall area and cornice, with their proportions carefully worked out according to set principles of design. Linenfold panelling went out of favour, but raised panels were still popular and the mouldings were quite bold in character, often projecting proud of the face of the framing members. At this period, too, pine and other softwoods began to replace

171

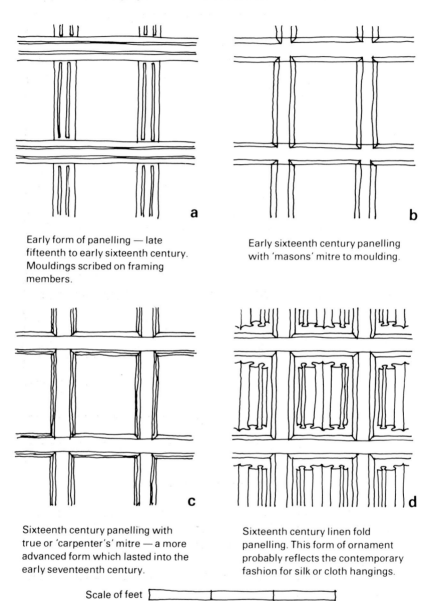

Early form of panelling — late fifteenth to early sixteenth century. Mouldings scribed on framing members.

Early sixteenth century panelling with 'masons' mitre to moulding.

Sixteenth century panelling with true or 'carpenter's' mitre — a more advanced form which lasted into the early seventeenth century.

Sixteenth century linen fold panelling. This form of ornament probably reflects the contemporary fashion for silk or cloth hangings.

Scale of feet

0   3

Fig. 50 **Panelling, typical early forms. At this period panelling was generally of oak. Sometimes decoration was applied, particularly in more ornamental forms.**

Scale of feet

0   5

Fig. 51 **Late seventeenth and early eighteenth century panelling**

oak in panelling, and this later panelling was generally painted (fig. 51). The fashion for stripped pine is comparatively modern, and the prominent graining of the wood tends to detract from the mouldings and detail of the panelling.

Throughout the eighteenth century the mouldings on panelling became less bold and more refined. In the late eighteenth century Gothic details sometimes appeared, but by this time panelling was being largely superseded by ornamental plasterwork, or by the recently introduced wallpapers. Sometimes the panelling was reduced to the dado, and this fashion continued into the nineteenth century. In small houses and cottages this often took the form of plain vertical boarding known as matchboarding.

When we look at panelling we must beware of using it as a firm way of dating the building. Panelling was often introduced into older buildings as part of an improvement scheme. Furthermore, it was often moved from one building to another, or refixed in another part of the same building. It is sometimes possible to see when this has been done, but even if the panelling was definitely made for its present position it is rarely possible to prove that it is part of the original construction.

Beams

The main beams supporting the upper floors can often provide useful dating information. The first thing to decide is whether the beams, and therefore the floor itself, are contemporary with the original structure, or later insertions. This may sometimes be seen from their relationship with the main framing in a timber-framed house, or to a chimney stack. If the floor is a later insertion, this could be evidence for an open hall, particularly if this is supported by features of the roof construction.

The design of the beams themselves may also be helpful. In the smallest houses and cottages they may be so plain and rough in outline as to be difficult to date, but where the outer corners have been chamfered, or splayed off, this feature can be used as a guide to dating. In the sixteenth century the chamfers were usually very deep, cutting away a considerable part of the beam. In later work the chamfers became progressively smaller (see fig. 21, page 70).

Generally the chamfer does not extend for the full length of the beam. It is 'stopped' just before it meets the wall. The details of these stops may also indicate the approximate date of the beam, the more elaborate stops generally being later than the plainer ones, although, in the simplest houses, plain stopped chamfers continued in use. In better-class houses, particularly in the more important rooms, the beams may be moulded, not simply chamfered, and these mouldings may also help to date the beams. In the earlier examples, fifteenth and early sixteenth century work, the mouldings are Gothic in character, while the later sixteenth and seventeenth century beams have mouldings showing the influence of classical design.

By the later seventeenth century ornamental plaster ceilings were becoming fashionable, and these sometimes concealed the main beams as well as the intermediate joists. By the eighteenth century exposed timber

A stop-chamfered beam
in the ceiling of a seven‐
teenth century house

beams were rare except in the smaller houses and cottages. Where the main beams could not be completely concealed they were usually cased in plaster or boarding, and finished with a cornice moulding continuous with that round the top of the walls. However, where possible, beams projecting below the ceiling line were avoided, the floor being constructed with separate ceiling joists, framed into the main beams independently of the floor joists above them.

In this way, many early beams were hidden during the eighteenth and nineteenth centuries. They may be revealed during modern alterations, and this can present a problem to the restorer, particularly if the room contains good Georgian panelling or other features. Should the older beams be exposed, perhaps involving the removal of an eighteenth century cornice, or should they be covered again to maintain the Georgian character of the room? It is not necessarily best to go back to the original in every case.

Staircases

The earliest staircases were little more than ladders, giving access to the lofts or upper rooms at the ends of the open halls. These stairs are unlikely to have survived. Next came the spiral or newel stair, generally sited next to the chimney stack, either in the centre of the house or on the gable wall. These might be of wood or stone. In medieval houses spiral stairs are sometimes found in the thickness of a wall, or in a circular or polygonal turret. Stone steps are of course of solid construction, and the earliest timber stairs were similar. Later came separate treads and risers, still much heavier in section than those of modern staircases, and generally of oak (figs. 52 and 53).

Historical survey of a house:

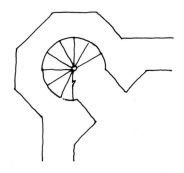

Circular newel stair or vice. Medieval.

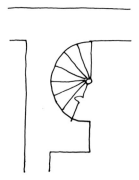

Semi-circular newel stair. Sixteenth and seventeenth centuries. Found in cottages until the nineteenth century.

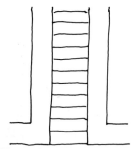

Straight flight between solid walls — from the sixteenth century.

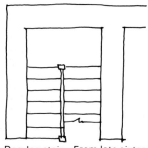

Dog-leg stair. From late sixteenth century, more common from seventeenth century.

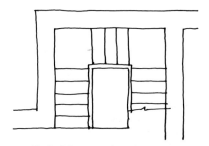

Stair rising round a solid core. Late sixteenth and early seventeenth century. In larger houses.

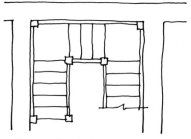

Open-well stair, from mid seventeenth century.

Fig. 52 **Staircases, plan types.**

Scale of feet

0   5   10

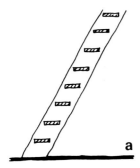

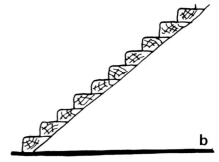

Early ladder type stair, medieval. Probably used later in cottages but few have survived.

Stair formed from solid baulks of timber, medieval to early sixteenth century — used later in poorer-type houses.

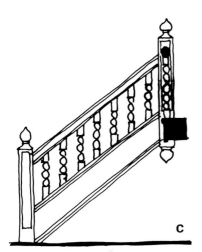

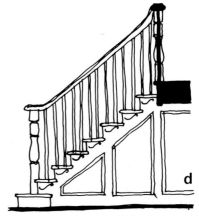

Closed-string stair with turned balusters. Sixteenth to early eighteenth century. Used first in larger houses. In smaller houses timbers are slighter and plainer.

Cut-string stair with plain slender balusters and panelled spandril. Late eighteenth and early nineteenth century. In smaller houses the closed-string stair survived longer, being simpler to construct.

Scale of feet

0   5

Fig. 53 **Staircases, construction.**

Historical survey of a house: The interior

The next development was the straight-flight or, depending on the space available, the 'dog-leg' stair, returning on itself with a landing halfway up the flight. These stairs first appeared in the late sixteenth or early seventeenth century in larger houses, but newel stairs continued to be constructed in smaller houses and cottages into the eighteenth and even the early nineteenth century in some areas.

The early dog-leg and straight-flight stairs had closed strings (the outer framing members), with the edges of the treads and risers framed into and concealed behind the strings. They were generally of oak, and the mouldings of the handrails, balusters and capping to the strings were often quite bold in character. The newel posts projected above the handrail, often with a carved or moulded cap, and projected below the strings with a similarly carved or moulded pendant.

A further development from the dog-leg stair was the open-well stair where the two flights were separated to give a more spacious effect. Sometimes this was taken further, with the stairs rising round the four sides of a square stairwell, with quarter space landings in the corners. In the larger houses the staircase was now designed as a focal feature of the entrance hall, sometimes with two flights leading down from a central upper landing.

An early seventeenth-century closed string stair, with heavy turned balusters, in process of restoration.

The Old Vicarage, Methwold, Norfolk. Wall paintings in an early sixteenth century house revealed during repairs. Note how the simulated studding is carried over the actual structural framing, i.e. the curved brace.

The closed-string stair continued in use in smaller houses, but elsewhere it was often superseded in the eighteenth century by the cut-string stair (fig. 53d). In this the string is cut away to allow the tread to project slightly beyond it, the nosing to the tread being returned at the side as a capping to the string. Balusters now became lighter in section, and the handrail was continued over the top of the newel, often being finished with a scroll or wreath.

Oak was still sometimes used, but by the eighteenth century imported mahogany had become popular for the handrail. The rest of the stair might also be of this material, but was often of softwood, and painted.

Wall plaster and decorations

Medieval plaster was generally composed of lime and sand only, and was applied quite thinly, following the contour of the wall surface. By the seventeenth century a thicker coat of plaster was used, often reinforced with goat or ox hair. The introduction of 'Roman cement' (a hard hydraulic lime) in the later eighteenth century, and of Portland cement in the nineteenth century, produced harder plasters often finished with a steel trowel to provide a smooth regular surface. A similar effect is obtained with the patent gypsum-based plasters used today.

These later plasters were often applied over the earlier coats, and successive layers may be revealed during repairs and alterations. There is a fashion today for leaving internal brick and stone walling exposed, particularly in medieval and Tudor houses, but this was not done when they were first built. Internal walls were almost invariably plastered unless they were of ashlar stone. Even this, like the plastered walls, was usually finished with limewash, and in all but the humblest houses often had painted decoration.

Early painted decoration, covered by successive layers of limewash and later plaster, may be discovered when work is carried out on old houses, and this is one reason why the removal of these later layers should be done with very great care. In many cases the later limewash has helped to preserve the decorations, and in the hands of an expert it can generally be removed without damaging the painting, but this is definitely not a task for the amateur, however enthusiastic. Specialist advice should always be obtained.

In medieval buildings the plaster was often marked out in imitation of ashlar stone. The same principle was sometimes followed in timber-framed buildings where the internal walls, plastered over completely, were then painted in imitation of timber-framing. In other cases textile hangings were depicted.

Apart from these attempts to emulate other materials and finishes, more frankly decorative paintings are also found, particularly in later medieval, Tudor and Stuart buildings. Floral designs, copies of architectural ornament, and figure subjects, often of a religious or allegorical character, as well as inscriptions and religious texts, all occur, particularly in houses of the more wealthy. The style of the architectural ornament and the costumes of the figure subjects will help to date these paintings, which may be later than the building itself. Incidentally, painted decoration may also be found on early panelling and ceiling beams — another reason why any cleaning should be carried out with great care.

By the end of the seventeenth century wall painting of this type was passing out of fashion, and it was often covered by later plaster or panelling.

Wallpapers were introduced into England during the eighteenth century, but were not common in smaller houses before the nineteenth century when cheaper production methods had been developed. The old paper was not always stripped when rooms were redecorated, and several layers of paper may be found when preparing a room for redecoration today. It will rarely be possible to preserve the early papers intact, but if a sufficient section of the earliest paper can be saved it may be possible to date it, at least approximately. The local museum will probably be able to help in this matter. As with other decorative finishes the oldest surviving wallpaper may well be considerably later in date than the house itself.

Having considered all these internal features of the house, and used them to help determine its age, we must always remember the possibility of components being re-used from other buildings. This is why their evidence must be considered in conjunction with that of the plan form and the roof structure. The plan form, if we can discover it, is almost bound to be authentic, and the roof structure, unless it has been completely renewed, which is soon apparent, is less likely than any other part of the house to have been tampered with. Any alterations to it are likely to be completely functional and honest, and to tell their own story.

The fact that some features of the house may have been brought from elsewhere does not necessarily detract from its interest. After the dissolution of the monasteries a good deal of material from the monastic buildings found its way into local houses, and castles damaged in the Civil War were another source of building material. If material in a house has obviously come from another building, it may be worth trying to trace its source.

Another thing we may find is the retention of certain structural features, generally the most durable and difficult to demolish, in houses which have otherwise been completely rebuilt. Often a house will be found to have a cellar of much earlier date than the main building, particularly in towns. Other features most often retained in this way are chimney stacks, especially the earlier, more massive ones. If a timber-framed house was burnt down, the brick chimneys often survived and were incorporated in the new building.

We must also, of course, remember the fact of architectural time-lag, and the difficulty this can pose in dating buildings from their details. In any area it is generally safe to say that one design of door, window, beam, etc., is earlier than another, but, as already explained, there may be a difference of as much as a hundred years between the dates of similar features in the south-east and the north-west parts of Britain. This is why it is so helpful if a typical building in a given area can be given a firm date, possibly from documentary evidence, as this can be used as a guide to dating other houses in that area.

A contrast between a largely unaltered cottage at Corfe
Castle, Dorset, below, and a 'period' reconstruction in
Broadway, Hereford and Worcestershire, above. Note the
difference in the scale of the windows.

9
Is it genuine?

In carrying out a survey of a house we have already seen the problems created by the re-use of components from other buildings, perhaps earlier buildings on the site. Until the late eighteenth century this was generally done for utilitarian reasons; materials were valuable in relation to the cost of labour, and it was therefore an economy to move windows, doors and timbers from a redundant building to one under construction or repair.

From the late eighteenth century onwards we find a new development, due to the growing interest in antiquarianism. Not only were older materials re-used, but new work was executed in conscious imitation of a past style. Sometimes this took the form of a 'restoration' (more or less conjectural) of vanished, or supposedly vanished features of the building. This process, which is still common among owners and repairers of old houses, adds to the problems of interpreting the history of the building. How can we tell whether what we are looking at is really of the age indicated by its general appearance?

The first thing to bear in mind is that the more we can study and familiarize ourselves with old houses which have not been treated in this way, the easier it will be to distinguish the genuine from the imitation. Although certain guidelines are given below, there is no doubt that in time one acquires a feeling for old buildings, and certain features will immediately arouse suspicions that all is not what it seems.

The extent of the problem can vary greatly. On the one hand we may have a house which has simply had a few features renewed in what an owner considered a correct sytle — 'Bringing it back to the original.' At the other extreme we may find a house newly built or rebuilt in a period style, possibly using a great deal of salvaged material, perhaps from an earlier house on the site. Alternatively, an old house may have had a new wing added in a reproduction style.

It is interesting that each age has had its own favourite reproduction style. In the late eighteenth and early nineteenth centuries a light-hearted

A modern 'Georgian' terrace at Frankwell, Shrewsbury.

form of Gothic was favoured, based on the late Gothic or early Tudor style, sometimes combined with some oriental motifs. In the mid nineteenth century this gave way to a rather hard, spiky Gothic, and a striving for historical accuracy; this hardness was accentuated by the use of machine-cut mouldings and ornament, and the substitution of pitch pine for oak in carpentry and joinery. In the Edwardian period a form of Baroque, known at the time as 'Queen Anne', but perhaps better described by Sir Osbert Lancaster as 'Pont Street Dutch', was much in favour for domestic work. This gave way in the 1920s and 1930s to a revived Tudor style, featuring half-timbering and diamond-paned leaded lights. This style is still popular, but in recent years it has to some extent been superseded by a revived Georgian, aided by the ease with which components approximating to eighteenth century originals may be mass-produced.

Let us deal first with the larger-scale problem, the 'reproduction' building, or part of a building, possibly re-using some old materials and components. Here we can probably rely on the two factors which I have stressed throughout this book as being of prime importance in dating a house: the plan form and the roof construction. However careful the reproduction in other ways, it is unlikely that the builder of a new house will have planned it on medieval or Tudor lines, or have constructed a cruck or crown post roof. Indeed, the hidden parts of the roof will probably be frankly modern. This could, of course, indicate a re-roofing of a genuine old building, but an examination of the roof space, if this is accessible, combined with a study of the plan form and the general proportions of the building, will usually reveal the truth.

Is it genuine?

A mock 'Georgian' door much in use today, with glazing in the form of a mock fanlight.

A careful study of the chimney stacks will also help us here. As we have seen, early stacks were very large, and while the builder of a Tudor style house may make a good attempt at reproducing an inglenook fireplace he is hardly likely to waste valuable floor space by building a chimney stack on the old scale. It is also worth checking the wall thicknesses, which in modern work are likely to be thinner than in old buildings of the same style.

Ceiling heights may also provide a clue. Until the later seventeenth century these were generally lower in smaller houses and cottages than those of today. Any reproduction house, or wing of a house, will probably have had to comply with the modern Building Regulations in this respect. This could also affect the sizes of windows, which are likely to be larger in relation to the wall area than in genuine small houses of the period.

In the case of a new wing added to an old house we should also ask ourselves why it was added, what extra accommodation it provides, and whether such an addition was typical of the period in question.

Even if a house has not been rebuilt or enlarged in recent times it may still have had a considerable amount of restoration, as distinct from straightforward repair or alterations to suit changing needs. The owner of, say, a Tudor house which has had a Georgian face-lift may decide to 'put it back as it was'. This could involve removal of external plaster, tile-hanging or weatherboarding, restoration of the old timber-framing, brick or rubble stone, and replacement of the inserted Georgian sash windows by Tudor-style mullioned windows. Sometimes this will have been done so crudely that it is immediately apparent, but in other cases careful inspection will be necessary to discover the truth. I list below a number of features which may have been 'restored', with some advice on how this may be discovered.

185

In this house at Lavenham, Suffolk, the timber framing was plastered over in the eighteenth or nineteenth century, and new windows inserted. Recently the plaster has been stripped, revealing the earlier blocked windows, but leaving the later ones intact, projecting beyond the wall face. This illustrates a common problem — how far should one take 'restoration' as distinct from straightforward repair?

Walling

Brickwork

As we have seen, early bricks were generally thinner and sometimes longer and wider than modern ones, and were often irregular in size and shape. Hand-made bricks of this type may still be obtained, and of course second-hand bricks are sometimes available. If the bricks themselves appear consistent with the apparent age of the building, note the bond used. Very early brickwork was often built in no regular bond. English Bond and its variations were usual until the second half of the seventeenth century (see page 146). After this, Flemish Bond was almost universal, except in nineteenth century engineering works, such as bridges, where the greater strength of English Bond was desirable. A wall of thin Tudor bricks built in Flemish Bond is immediately suspect, as is the use of Stretcher Bond, which probably indicates modern cavity walling.

Timber-framing

This material is much subject to restoration. As we have seen, timbers were often re-used from earlier buildings for economic reasons, and such

The light timber-framing of this eighteenth century house at Lavenham was almost certainly plastered over when it was first built. The current fashion for exposed timber-framing has resulted in the stripping of the plaster. Would the original builders of the house have wanted this effect?

timbers were generally used structurally. When 'old oak beams' have been inserted purely for effect, they are often not jointed to the main timbers, as may be seen from a careful examination. Sometimes they may be only thin boards fixed on to the face of the wall.

Timber-framing in a style not typical of the area, or of the apparent date of the house, should also be regarded with suspicion. It may be an exceptional example of an alien form, and thus of great interest, but it is more likely to be a fake.

As already mentioned, when timber frames were made up in the carpenter's yard the members to be framed together were identified by Roman numerals. When these are found to be out of sequence, or the numbers in a truss do not match, it is likely that the original framing has been dismantled and re-assembled, or even that the present structure has been made up of separate timbers from elsewhere.

Modern inserted timbers are often easily distinguished by the fact that they have been machine-cut and sawn, contrasting with the earlier hand-wrought work where the adze was used, which produced a slightly irregular surface. However, modern timbers are sometimes exaggeratedly adzed to give an 'antique' effect. With experience this is equally easy to distinguish from authentic early timberwork.

In the late seventeenth and eighteenth centuries old timber-framing was often covered, partly for reasons of fashion, and partly because it and the

187

old infilling had ceased to be weatherproof. The lighter framing used in buildings of these later periods was nearly always covered from the start. In recent times much of this timbering has been stripped, and this often necessitates a good deal of renewal. One may even find a timber-framed house, subsequently plastered over, which has had mock half-timbering painted on the face of the plaster, or thin boards nailed on this in imitation of the original framing.

Stone

The character of stone walling, whether ashlar or rubble, should be noted. If the stone is not local, could it have been brought to the site before the days of cheap transport? Does it appear to have been re-used from another building? Does the method of laying the stone accord with other local examples of the period?

As with brickwork, the pointing may indicate the age of the wall if the original pointing has survived. Before the nineteenth century this was usually in lime mortar, using rather a coarse, gritty sand, although a smooth, fine-jointed pointing was sometimes used in the eighteenth century in more formal work. In many cases, however, the wall will have been repointed, making it look newer than it is.

As mentioned in Chapter 7, rubble stone was often limewashed externally, until the nineteenth century when it was generally cleaned off. It is difficult, however, to remove limewash completely. If a stone wall retains traces of limewash it is unlikely to have been restored or rebuilt in recent times.

Plaster

If this is of the right apparent age for the house, this should confirm the building's authenticity (see page 179). It should also be easy to see where door and window openings have been inserted or blocked. Often, though, plaster will have been renewed and in these cases it is not on its own a reliable guide to dating. The same is generally true of other applied facings such as tile-hanging and weatherboarding.

It is sometimes possible to see whether tile-hanging is recent or has been renewed (possibly re-using the old tiles) by examining the external angles of the walls. In old work the tiles were simply cut and fitted together, or covered with timber fillets. Today, specially made angle tiles are generally used, providing a more weathertight finish.

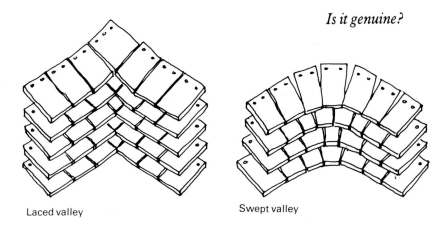

Laced valley   Swept valley

Fig. 54 **Traditional valley treatments in tiles and stone slates**

Roofs

As mentioned before, roof coverings are easily renewed, and are not in themselves an infallible guide to dating. Old tiles, stone slates or true slates on a roof may have been brought from elsewhere. Apart from this possibility, an old roof may have been stripped and re-covered, re-using the original or similar old materials. There are a number of differences between older and more modern practice which may help us to see whether this has been done, as described below.

Verges Until the nineteenth century, the bonding of the tile and slate courses was obtained by using half-tiles or slates at the roof edges or verges. In modern practice, 'tile and half' or 'slate and half' tiles and slates are used, giving a stronger and more weather-resistant finish.

Valleys In old houses, valleys were usually 'swept' or 'laced' in better-class work, shaping the tiles and working them round the junction of the two roofs, while in poorer houses the tiles or slates were simply cut, mitred and fitted together on the line of the valley. By the eighteenth century valleys were often formed in lead. Today, purpose-made valley tiles are most commonly used, although laced or swept valleys are occasionally found in good quality work (fig 54). Like the tile and half tiles, the new valley tiles may not be an exact match for the old tiles used on the rest of the roof. In slate roofs today, lead valleys are nearly always used.

Hips On old tiled roofs these were usually finished with 'bonnet' hip tiles, which are still common today. On stone slate and true slate roofs the slates might be cut and fitted together, or covered with specially cut stone or slate hips, similar to those used on the ridge. In the eighteenth and nineteenth centuries, ridges and hips on slate and tile roofs were often covered with lead. Half-round ridge tiles were also used on the hips, particularly in the nineteenth and early twentieth centuries. Today, slate roofs generally have Blue Staffordshire tile ridges and hips, in an attempt to match the colour of the slating.

In the nineteenth century machine-made tiles were introduced. These are generally smoother and flatter than the old hand-made tiles, and more regular in size and shape. Hand-made tiles are still produced, similar in general appearance to the old tiles but, also, rather more regular in shape. Some modern tiles are artificially stained to give a weathered or antique appearance. The old tiles were not treated in this way, and their mellow appearance is the result of natural weathering over the centuries. A close inspection will usually reveal the difference.

If it appears that a roof has been relaid either with new or re-used old materials, we can only tell whether it is authentic by examining the roof structure. Apart from these problems, we may find that an early roof has been embellished in the nineteenth century with the ornamental ridge tiles and carved or moulded bargeboards popular in new houses of the period. This again emphasizes the dangers of a superficial inspection when trying to date a house.

Windows

These are easily altered, both by those who want to modernize a house and those who want to 'restore' it to its original or presumed original condition.

First examine the head, jambs and cill, to see whether it appears that the window was formed as the house was built, or is a later insertion. The latter often involves some disturbance of the walling.

The type of window most likely to have been 'restored' in this way is the stone or timber mullioned window typical of the sixteenth and seventeenth centuries, probably with leaded lights. Occasionally, genuine old windows have been re-used from elsewhere. In such cases we can only compare their style with that of the rest of the house, and look for signs that the walling has been disturbed. Victorian or modern copies are usually easier to detect. The mullions and surrounds, whether of stone or timber, being machine-cut are rather hard and mechanical in appearance, and are sometimes slighter in section than those in old windows. The mullions themselves are often spaced farther apart. Indeed, today, standard Tudor-

Cottages at Broadway, Hereford and Worcestershire. The original stone mullioned windows survive on the ground floor, but the first-floor dormers have been replaced with modern casements of a common standard design.

style windows are made to accommodate standard metal casements fitted with leaded lights. In old windows the fixed lights are glazed directly to the mullions and surrounds, and the opening lights have flat section wrought-iron frames with hand-made fasteners, unlike the modern 'Z' section metal windows. In modern work, leaded lights are sometimes fitted into timber opening sashes; this is rarely found in genuine early windows.

In old leaded windows the panes are usually rectangular and are sometimes slightly irregular in shape. Diamond panes are occasionally found, as are other more ornamental patterns, but these are more likely to be Victorian or modern. The glass in old leaded windows often has a slightly irregular surface, perhaps with a few air bubbles, and is sometimes a light green or yellow tint, due to impurities in the material. Modern glass is either flat sheet glass, or a mock antique glass with an exaggerated textured surface.

Georgian sash windows are less often restored although they may be inserted today in Victorian buildings. They are quite likely to be modern standard products, and are usually easy to recognise by their regular lines and their details, including the glazing bars, when compared with genuine eighteenth century examples. It is worth examining the glass in any supposedly Georgian windows. Genuine ones would originally have been

191

glazed in crown glass, which, having been blown into a sphere and then flattened, is not completely flat and produces a slight wave or distortion. Some, at least, of this glass may have survived. In Georgian bow windows, a favourite subject for restoration, the glass was generally curved to follow the plane of the window. This is rarely done today.

Beware of 'bottle glass' or 'bull's eyes'. Originally these were simply the point where the glass blower's rod was broken off the centre of the crown glass sphere — almost a waste product. They were used in the cheapest houses, in the less important rooms, and the centre where the rod was broken off may have quite rough edges. Modern purpose-made copies are smoother and more regular in appearance.

Doors and doorways

As with windows, the most popular subject for restoration is the Tudor door, generally of oak. Sometimes we even see these inserted in Georgian and Victorian houses. The modern standard doors of this type are very light and flimsy compared with authentic ones, and are usually easily recognisable. Sometimes, however, a more solid door is found, perhaps made up from old material to give it a more weathered appearance. Here an examination of the ironwork may help. The early doors were hung not on modern type hinges, but on iron pins or rides, fixed directly either to the stone jambs, to the main framing of a timber-framed house or, particularly from the seventeenth century, to a heavy oak frame. The wide iron strap hinges were necessary to support the weight of the door. Modern reproduction doors are rarely hung in this way. Strap hinges may be used, but we sometimes find normal butt hinges with mock straps fixed to the face of the door. Modern reproduction ironwork sometimes has an artificially hammered surface to produce an antique effect.

Georgian-style doors are popular today, and many standard types are made. Some of these in fact bear little resemblance to any known originals, but others are reasonably authentic in design. Generally, except in small houses with narrow entrance halls, old doors are wider in relation to their height than more modern ones. As well as the doors themselves, standard Georgian-style door canopies and surrounds are now mass-produced, sometimes in fibreglass. A careful examination will reveal these.

In deciding whether a door is authentic, it is of course important to note whether it is in the normal position for a house of its type. In a timber-framed house, the original position of a door can often be found by the absence of peg-holes and mortices for intermediate horizontal members in the upright timbers forming the door opening. Sometimes, evidence for a former door head may be seen. If the present door is not in its original position, it may simply have been moved intact, but its authenticity must be questioned.

Interiors

Ceiling beams and joists

Internally, the favourite subjects for restoration are probably ceiling beams and joists, the 'old oak beams' that feature so often in estate agents' descriptions. Here genuine material may have been brought from elsewhere. Beams should be examined to see whether they fit their sites. Do the 'stops' at the ends of the chamfers come in the right position? Is the spacing of the beams logical, and consistent with the plan and structure of the house, or are they simply placed for effect? Completely new beams may be identified by a machine-sawn or self-consciously adzed surface.

Exposed ceiling joists should be examined. Where these were originally intended to be exposed, they were usually carefully finished, being chamfered, or even moulded in the best quality work. After the mid to late seventeenth century the joists were normally covered by a plaster ceiling, and were therefore more roughly finished. They were also by this time often of softwood rather than oak, and were deeper and narrower than the earlier joists. At this period, too, older oak joists were sometimes covered with plaster ceilings to reflect the current fashion.

As with timber-framed walls, many joists have been uncovered in recent restorations and in the case of the later buildings this uncovering has often revealed rather rough and flimsy joists, generally of softwood and not originally intended to be seen. Sometimes these have been stained in imitation of oak, covered with oak boards or oak-faced plywood, or even replaced by oak joists from elsewhere. In extreme cases the desire for 'old oak beams' has resulted in planks being fixed to the underside of a plaster ceiling, performing no structural function.

Cornices and plasterwork

Here Georgian detail is easily reproduced and standard mass-produced sections are available. These may sometimes be distinguished by their very regular lines, the way the sections are joined together and by the fact that they may appear to be simply planted on to an older plaster ceiling.

Is it genuine?

Panelling

Panelling is so easily moved from one position to another that it is rarely a reliable guide to dating the building. Modern reproduction panelling, like other timberwork, is generally either obviously machine-sawn and finished or artificially adzed to produce an antique effect.

Fireplaces

Over the centuries most of the large old open fireplaces were partly built up to take smaller grates. Recently many of them have been opened up again. Sometimes this has been done without disturbing the original structure, much of which survives intact, but difficulties sometimes arise, perhaps because an original timber lintel has been removed or cut away, and the brick or stone jambs damaged for a later fireplace. In these cases the re-opened inglenook fireplace may be largely a reconstruction, and should be carefully examined.

Later, Georgian-type fireplaces and surrounds are often moved from one house to another, and there are many modern reproductions, some quite convincing in design. Sometimes when a fireplace of this type has been fixed in a new position, it has been necessary to piece in the skirting and any dado or panelling on each side of it. This can be seen by a careful inspection. A Victorian fireplace is likely to be authentic, though of course possibly later than the building. They are not yet sufficiently fashionable to be subjects for restoration.

From this chapter it might appear that the dating of a house is an almost impossible task, when the problems of faking and reproduction are added to all the others. I would emphasize again, however, that the more we can study genuine unspoiled houses the more easily we shall be able to distinguish between them and their imitations. This cannot be learnt from books or from photographs. We must get out and absorb the atmosphere of the houses themselves, and making a careful measured survey is one of the best ways of achieving this.

10
Take this house

The nineteenth century brick facade hides a timber-framed open hall house

18 and 19, West Orchard, Dorset

This house illustrates the danger of judging a building by a superficial external inspection only. At first sight, although pleasant enough, it does not appear to be of any particular historic interest. It is built of red brick, with a thatched roof, and is of two storeys. All the windows are comparatively recent, and the two adjoining front doors might indicate that it is, and perhaps always has been, two attached but not identical cottages.

Looking at the front (north) elevation, the positions of the two chimney stacks — one to the left of the eastern door and the other on the west gable wall — might suggest that the building may originally have been a single house of the three-room and cross-passage plan, and the presence of the attached farm buildings to the south and west show that it was once a farmhouse, later sold off from the farm itself. However, from what can be seen from the front there is little to contradict the dating given in the original description of the house, in the Supplementary List of Buildings of Special Architectural or Historic Interest, as 'early nineteenth century'. This, and the fact that the house does not appear at all in the Survey of the Royal Commission on Historical Monuments (Dorset Vol. IV. North), also might well suggest that it is of no special historic interest.

On walking round to the rear of the house, however, a completely different picture starts to appear. The east gable wall is weatherboarded, above a later lean-to addition, a strange feature in a brick house, and on the rear wall the eaves of the thatched roof are at about first-floor level. The pitch of the main rear roof slope is therefore much steeper than that of the front slope. It appears that the front wall has been raised, and the roof pitch flattened, to improve the headroom in the first-floor rooms. Since the brickwork of the front wall appears to be all of one date, the fact that this wall has been raised now indicates that the brickwork is a later refacing, or reconstruction of an earlier structure, and that the house itself may be of much earlier origin than is suggested by its first appearance.

All this is confirmed by an internal inspection. From this, and from a

The low eaves at the rear of the house indicate its possible early origin

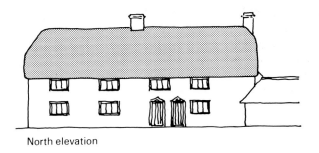

North elevation

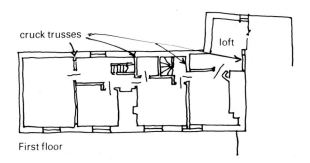

First floor

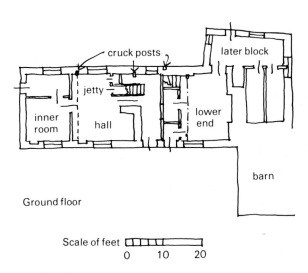

Ground floor

Scale of feet

0   10   20

Fig. 55 **18 and 19 West Orchard, as existing.**

197

measured survey, it becomes apparent that the two cottages were indeed originally one house; that the original structure was timber-framed, of true cruck construction, and that the house was of the late medieval or early Tudor long-house type, with an open hall.

Of the two external door openings in the front wall the easternmost one is the original entrance, the other having been formed when the house was divided into two cottages. Evidence for the original timber-framed structure survives in the weatherboarded east gable wall and at the top of the west end of the rear (south) wall, now visible in the roof space. The house is divided into four bays by three true cruck trusses. There is a similar truss in the west gable (partly destroyed when the later chimney stack was inserted here). These trusses are numbered 1 to 4 on the plan and in the following description. The construction of the east gable, which is half-hipped, could not be seen, but it may incorporate base crucks.

The present plan comprises, from east to west:

1   An inner room of one bay, divided from the hall by a partition, partly of plank and muntin construction, and partly of later studding. This partition is set about 1 foot 3 inches east of truss no. 1 and the ceiling in this narrow section is about 6 inches lower than the rest of the present hall ceiling. This suggests the presence of an internal jetty, in the house as first built.

2   A hall of one bay, now containing a large inserted stone chimney stack.

3   A cross passage of half a bay, separated from the hall by the chimney stack and by an inserted staircase, and from the lower end by a partition, now plastered, and showing evidence of a blocked door opening.

4   A lower end of one and a half bays, with a large stone inserted chimney stack replacing most of the original gable wall.

To the south and west of this part of the house is a stone-built extension, providing additional kitchen and service accommodation, with a barn, now in separate ownership, on the north.

There are signs of smoke-blackening on the truss in the west gable (no. 4) and on the adjoining truss (no. 3), i.e. that in the lower end. Apart from this section, the trusses and other roof timbers are not visible above first-floor ceiling level. The upper part of the truss between the hall and the inner room (no. 1) appears to have been closed, since a collar beam about 3 feet 6 inches above the present first-floor level has been cut away for a door opening. This indicates that the first-floor room (the solar) was not open to the hall, and must have been reached by a stair from the inner

The cruck truss between the hall and the cross passage

room. The smoke-blackening on trusses 3 and 4 suggests that the rest of the house was originally open to the roof. If there were partitions separating the hall and the lower end from the cross passage they would have extended only to about eaves height, i.e. to the level of the present first-floor.

It would therefore appear that the original form of the house was as follows (looking at it from east to west):

1 An inner room of one bay, with an attic room over, separated from the hall by partitions on each floor, the first floor being jettied and projecting about 1 foot 3 inches into the hall. This jetty might have formed a canopy over the upper end of the hall. There may even have been a slightly raised floor here echoing the raised dais found in the hall of the typical manor house, but no evidence for this survives. The inner room may have been a parlour, or sleeping room or a service room, and the room above it either a sleeping room or a store. Both these rooms were, and still are, unheated.

2 A hall of one bay, heated by an open hearth. There may have been a partition in truss no. 2 or in its lower part, but no firm evidence of this can be seen.

3 A lower end of two bays, with a pair of opposed doors in its eastern section, forming a cross passage. It is not possible to say whether the

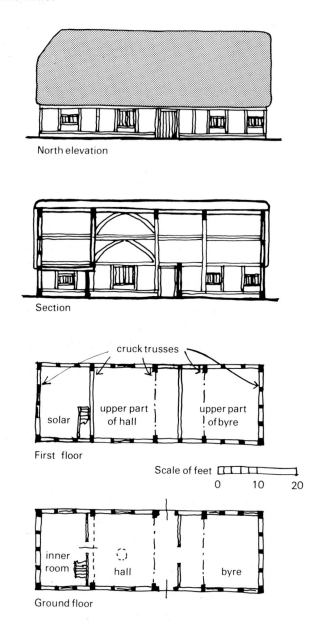

North elevation

Section

cruck trusses

solar

upper part of hall

upper part of byre

First floor

Scale of feet

0   10   20

inner room

hall

byre

Ground floor

Fig. 56 **18 and 19 West Orchard, probable original form.**

partition separating the cross passage from the rest of the lower end is original, but if there was a partition here it cannot have extended for the full height of the building, as is proved by the smoke-blackening on trusses nos 3 and 4.

The size of this lower end would be unusually large for a service room, or for the pantry and buttery arrangement of the Wealden house. In any case such service rooms were normally floored over, with storage rooms above them, and apart from the evidence of the smoke-blackening, this does not seem to have been the case here, since the main first-floor beam is not framed into the cruck truss. This suggests that the first floor here is a later insertion. Since the chimney stack in the west gable is also an insertion, the room is not likely to have originated as a kitchen, and it therefore seems to have had some non-domestic use, such as a byre. Indeed, if the present partition between this area and the cross passage is original, the built-up opening, which from the positions of peg-holes in the upper beam would have been about 4 feet wide, could well have been formed to allow access for animals, or for some bulky equipment other than normal domestic furnishings. This interpretation is also supported by the fact that the cross passage is outside the hall, as shown by its siting in relation to the eastern truss of the hall (no. 3).

As far as the possible date of the building is concerned, it is unlikely that an open hall would have been built after the middle of the sixteenth century. True cruck construction, of which comparatively few examples have been found in Dorset, also suggests a date no later than this.

At this original stage, the windows of the house would have been unglazed, probably with plain timber mullions and internal shutters. The first major improvement was the insertion of the large stone chimney stack in the hall, providing a more efficient form of heating than the old open hearth. The hall was probably floored over at the same time, both to facilitate heating and to provide an additional upper room. At about the same time the byre seems to have been converted into a kitchen, inserting the large gable end stack, and constructing a first floor, as in the hall. The animals would by now have been rehoused in a separate building.

The extension to the south and west of the house probably followed soon after to provide additional service rooms linked to the new kitchen. The inner room was probably by now used either as a parlour or a sleeping room and was still unheated. All this work probably took place during the seventeenth century, a period of prosperity when many older farmhouses were rebuilt or altered.

The last major change took place in the late eighteenth or early

Take this house

nineteenth century, when most of the external walls were rebuilt in brick and the front wall raised, flattening the roof pitch, to provide improved headroom at the front of the first-floor rooms. The division of the house into two units was a comparatively recent development, and has resulted in little structural alteration.

The house is thus a very interesting example of an early open hall house of the long-house type, being adapted and modernized to suit the changing needs and ideas of successive generations while still retaining much of its original plan form and structure. The fact that this course was chosen, rather than complete demolition and rebuilding at any time, must indicate continuous occupation as well as the basic soundness and adaptability of the original building.

It will be appreciated that the inspection of this house was carried out while it was occupied, and that no disturbance of the structure was involved. It is always possible that further investigation, including opening up and inspecting the rest of the roof space, would provide additional evidence, and might affect this interpretation of the history of the house.

Prinkham, Chiddingstone, Kent. Before recent repairs: much of the framing concealed by tile-hanging.

Prinkham, Chiddingstone, Kent

This house was included in the Provisional List of Buildings of Special Architectural or Historic Interest prepared in 1949, and confirmed in the Statutory List issued in 1954. The description, based on an external survey only, was as follows:

> Prinkham, near Bassetts Mill (sometimes called Packenham). Sixteenth century framed cottage with exposed half-timbering and rendered infilling. Good south elevation probably early seventeenth century with oversailing first floor with finely carved corner brackets and vertical half-timbering above. Oversailing gable end supported on carved brackets with pendants. Moulded barge boards with top centre pendant. Two storeys and gable end attic window. Leaded casement windows. Ground-floor bay window and first-floor window above with moulded mullions and transoms. Ridge tile roof with one end hipped and centre ridge stack. In very poor state of repair.

It will be seen that while the visible external features are described in some detail no attempt is made to describe the plan form or to interpret the history of the development of the house. The opportunity to survey and

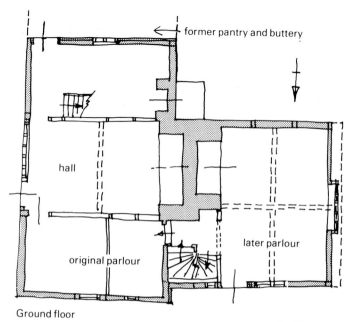

Fig. 57 **Plans, as existing**

Exterior showing the different forms of timber-framing in the two wings

record the house arose during the carrying out of repairs and alterations in 1968 and 1969. This work revealed a number of features which might otherwise not have been discovered.

The house stands in an isolated position between Chiddingstone and Cowden. It was probably built by a well-to-do yeoman farmer, and would originally have been surrounded by farm buildings, all of which have disappeared. They may have been of less permanent and substantial construction than the house. In Kent in the late medieval and Tudor periods isolated holdings of this type were common.

The plan of the house is T-shaped. As usual in this part of Kent it is built of timber-framing, although much of this was covered later with plaster and tile-hanging before the recent work was carried out. From an external inspection of the visible timbers it appeared that the two sections, the head and the stem of the T, were of different dates. The main wing (the head) was built with large panel framing, while that of the stem was of close studding, indicating a probable later date for this section.

The end (west) wall of the later wing had double jetties, at first and attic floor levels and, taking advantage of the fall in the ground level, this wing also had a cellar. The north wall of the older wing, the only wall in this

204

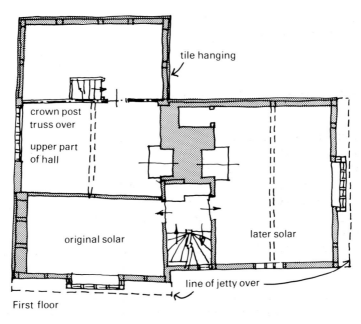

tile hanging

crown post
truss over

upper part
of hall

original solar

later solar

line of jetty over

First floor

Scale of feet

0   10   20

Take this house

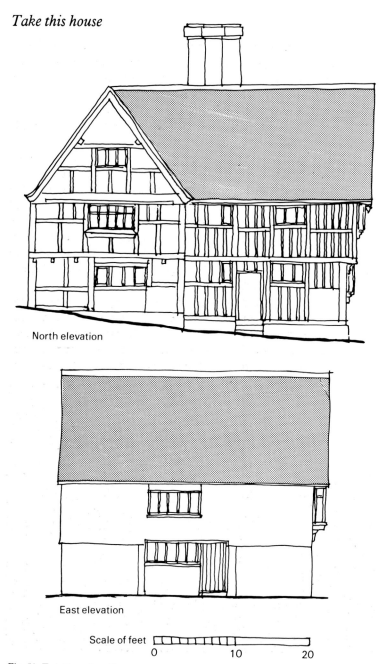

North elevation

East elevation

Scale of feet

0   10   20

Fig. 58 **Existing elevations**

wing with exposed timber-framing was jettied at attic level only, but at first-floor level the exposed ends of joists flush with the wall face suggested that there may once have been a jetty here, the wall having been rebuilt up to first-floor level flush with the upper wall.

The roofs were tiled with old plain tiles, and were all gabled, with moulded bargeboards. There was a large brick chimney stack, apparently of late sixteenth century date, at the junction of the two wings.

The general quality of the later wing appeared high. The exposed timbering was substantial, and on the ground and first floors there were oriel windows with moulded cills and ovolo moulded mullions. Most of the leaded lights had survived, some retaining early glass. The jetties had moulded fascias, and were supported on shaped brackets. There was a similar oriel window on the first floor of the north gable wall of the older wing, and the gable bargeboard and attic floor jetty here were all of similar detail to those in the later wing. This suggested that the older wing had been given a face-lift when the later wing was built.

An internal inspection and further inspection during the progress of the work revealed the development of the house. The earlier wing comprised the hall and one two-storeyed end of a late fifteenth century Wealden house. The hall was of two bays, with a central crown post and tie-beam truss, and a trussed rafter roof, all heavily smoke-blackened. Clearly the

Crown post roof of the hall of the older wing

hall had originally been open to the roof and heated by a central hearth, although it had been floored over completely at first floor, and partly at attic floor level. North of the hall was the solar block, with an original first floor, and an attic floor, probably inserted. The southern half of the hall had been partitioned off at ground and upper floor levels, and these partitions appeared contemporary with the flooring over of the hall. There were no signs of a screens passage, and the positions of the original entrance doors could not be traced, since the external walls had been rebuilt in brick up to first-floor level. There was also no evidence at this stage for a pantry and buttery block. The south wall had been rebuilt in brick up to first-floor level, and was covered with tile-hanging above this.

The later wing had been added in the late sixteenth or early seventeenth century, to provide additional living and sleeping accommodation. The chimney stack was inserted at the same time. The new wing contained a heated parlour on the ground floor, with bedrooms on the two upper floors reached by a new oak newel staircase. The old hall, now floored over, had been demoted to a kitchen, heated from the new chimney stack, the southern half of this room being partitioned off, presumably to form a pantry, while the old parlour may also now have been used as a service room. The old solar, now entered from the new staircase landing, was also probably a sleeping room at this time. It had been fitted with a new oriel window matching those in the new wing, probably replacing an old unglazed window. The original hipped roof over this room had been reconstructed as a jettied gable, also matching the gable in the new wing. The new room above the northern part of the old hall was heated from the main chimney stack, and was also presumably now a sleeping room.

At the time the recent repairs were started the house had been divided into two cottages, and it was not easy to see where the main entrance had been after the late Tudor alterations. There was an external door into the new parlour, but this, even if it was original, was unlikely to have been the main entrance. There was also an external door into the old hall (now the kitchen), but again it is not likely that a house of this quality would have had its main entrance in that position.

As mentioned previously, the lower part of the north wall of the older wing had at some time been rebuilt flush with the upper wall, doing away with the jetty there. It is therefore possible that there had been an entrance door there, turning the old parlour into an entrance hall rather than a service room. (This arrangement has been followed in the recent restoration.)

In the west wall of the old solar, adjoining the Tudor staircase, evidence

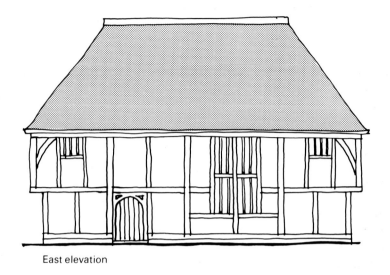

East elevation

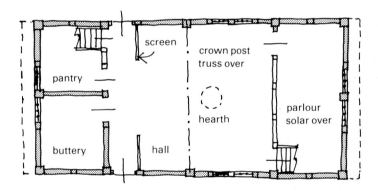

Fig. 59 **Prinkham, Chiddingstone, probable original form.**

was found for a late medieval unglazed window, and it is probable that all the original windows in this part of the house were of this type. Even more significant, when an opening was being formed for a new window in the south gable wall of the older wing (i.e. the south wall of the original hall) evidence was found for two doorways, almost certainly leading to a vanished pantry and buttery block. This had presumably been demolished when the new wing was added. It now appeared that the original house had been of the typical Wealden form, but with the parlour and pantry blocks jettied at their ends and not, as was more usual, at the front and rear of the house.

After the addition of the new wing in the late sixteenth or early seventeenth century (a time of considerable prosperity in Kent) little appears to have been done to the house apart from the later division into two cottages. It must have ceased to be the house of a separate farmstead, and the farm buildings were probably demolished or allowed to decay at the same time. This amalgamation of farms to form larger units was common in Kent, particularly during the eighteenth century. In the case of Prinkham, this probably accounts for the survival of the house to a large extent in its late Tudor form.

During this intervening period, up to the present day, only basic repairs seem to have been carried out. Much of the external walling was covered with tile-hanging, to save the cost of repairing the timbers and infilling. The fact that so much of the structure survived is a tribute to its quality.

When the List of Buildings of Special Architectural or Historic Interest was revised in 1975 the description of the house was amended to include some of the internal features, and to note that it incorporated part of an early hall house.

The following documentary evidence about this house exists in the Kent County Record Office:

The land in which Prinkham is situated, including most of the Parishes of Chiddingstone and Cowden, was acquired in the sixteenth century by the Streatfeilds, a yeoman family who eventually became substantial land-owners. The Streatfeild family records include a Settlement of some land in Chiddingstone Parish on Joan Basset of Chiddingstone, a widow, by Henry Streatfeild of Chiddingstone (described as a woollen draper), in 1590. The Settlement mentions land only, and does not refer to any buildings. As the earliest surviving part of Prinkham was probably built by this time, it may not have been included in the Settlement, but it is perhaps significant that the Bassett family subsequently owned the house, and there is a Bassett Mill nearby. The enlargement of the house dates from about this time.

The next relevant document, the first referring to the house by name, is a record of a legal dispute, dated 1680, concerning 'A farm called

Prinkham' in Chiddingstone Parish. Next we have the will of Michael Bassett, of Cowden, dated 1734 and proved in November 1736, which contains the following entry:

> Whereas I settled in marriage upon my dear and loving wife Elizabeth for the term of her natural life five full parts out of six full and equal parts of my farm and lands called or known by the name of Prinkham Farm lying and being in the several Parishes of Chiddingstone in the County of Kent and Withyham in the County of Sussex now my will is and I do hereby give and bequeath to my said wife Elizabeth the other said remaining sixth part of the said Prinkham Farm so that she shall enjoy and possess the said farm during the term of her natural life. . . [then follow monetary bequests to and provision for his daughters]. . . Item. I give devise and bequeath all the said Prinkham Farm with the appurtenances from and after the decease of the said Elizabeth my wife. unto my son Michael Bassett and his heirs.

A life interest in the property was thus left to Elizabeth Bassett, with her son Michael as the eventual heir. However, in January 1757 a further document records that Elizabeth Bassett leased Prinkham for a first payment of five shillings, and an annual peppercorn rent thereafter, to John Burgiss, John Saxby and William Everest. The property then comprised 80 acres of arable, meadows, pasture, orchards and wood, and, apart from the house, there were barns, stables, outhouses and other buildings. At that time the farm was occupied by Matthew Everest. His relation to William is not clear. If the property was intended to provide Elizabeth Bassett with an income for life it is not clear why she apparently disposed of it for a minimal profit. It may have been exchanged for other property of which no record exists here. Whatever happened, the Bassett family now disappear from the scene.

In his will of 1785, proved in 1790, John Saxby (one of the three lessees) devised Prinkham to his son Michael Saxby who was by then the occupant, in succession to Matthew Everest who had died in 1774. In the Tithe Map and Apportionment of circa 1840 Prinkham is shown owned by James Marchant and occupied by Richard Marchant. It is still shown as a separate farm unit, but the Marchants owned a considerable amount of other property in the Parish and may not have lived at Prinkham, which could have been let to sub-tenants.

An Agreement of November 1866 records that Richard Marchant agrees to let George Jenner an 'Apartment' of Prinkham House and two gardens at the rent of £2.2s5d per quarter. George Jenner was to keep the window glass and garden fences in good repair, 'The ovens door mantel shelf settle and part of old settle in kitchen and bench and shutter in pantry to belong to the said Richard Marchant'. A similar Agreement of Michaelmas, 1870 records that Richard Marchant agrees to let Edward Pearson a 'Tenement' of Prinkham House and garden at £5 per year. Edward Pearson was likewise to keep the window glass and garden fences in good repair and not to take in any person to live with him without the approval of the said Richard Marchant, 'the lock to the front door mantel shelf two small shelves and iron back and iron plate to kitchen fireplace ovens door and shelf in pantry to belong to the said Richard Marchant.'

This probably dates the division of the house into two cottages and its separation from the farm land. The remains of the 'settle and part of old settle in the kitchen' were still in the house when the recent repairs were put in hand.

In 1873 the property, described as 'formerly in the tenure or occupation of Matthew Everest, afterwards of Michael Saxby, afterwards of the said Charles Marchant, James Marchant otherwise James Marchant Hooker and Richard Marchant their undertenants or assigns' was conveyed by Messrs Marchant to the Trustees of the Waldo Settled Estates.

21 and 23, Cinderhills Road, Holmfirth, West Yorkshire

This exterior view shows the added external staircase and entrance to the first floor of No. 23. In No. 21 this feature has subsequently been removed. In both houses the original mullioned windows survive. In the adjoining houses they have been altered to take modern casements.

These houses are of more recent origin than the first two described in this chapter, and there is some available documentary evidence for their building and subsequent history. They are part of a terrace of four weavers' houses, Nos. 17, 19, 21 and 23, Cinderhills Road, which were built for letting by Joseph Beaumont, a cordwainer (cobbler), in or soon after 1794.

The village of Holmfirth, in the Holme valley, about six miles south of Huddersfield, was a centre of the cloth industry in the eighteenth century. At that time, weaving was still largely a cottage industry, unlike spinning which was by then mostly carried out in factories or workshops. A number of the weavers' houses have survived, with their typical long mullioned

213

windows in the upper storeys, lighting the weaving rooms. Holmfirth was part of the Parish of Kirkburton, in the Manor of Wakefield, which covered a large part of the former West Riding of Yorkshire, and survived from its origins in the Middle Ages into the 1930s, an unusually late date. Many of the manorial records still exist, including the Court Rolls, and later documents dating from the 1920s onwards relating to the extinguishment of the Manor and the enfranchisement of the manorial properties. Some early deeds of the Cinderhills Road houses have also survived. This property may serve as an example of what one can discover from documentary evidence: 200 years are covered, giving details of ownership, family relationships and, to some extent, the occupations of the people who lived in the houses.

An entry in the manorial Court Roll records that at the Court Baron held at Wakefield on 1 February, 1788, Joseph Beaumont, cordwainer, purchased (copyhold) land 'at or near Cinderhills' in Holmfirth from Joshua Cuttell, clothier, and William Walker, butcher. The price paid for all this land, which probably included the future sites of the four houses, was £215 and the annual rent to the Lord of the Manor was one shilling. The next relevant entry in the Court Roll records that at the Court Baron held at Wakefield on 14 March in the same year Joseph Beaumont and his wife Martha, as co-owners, mortgaged part of this land, amounting to six acres, to Abraham Thomas, gentleman, of Huddersfield, for £100. It may well be that this mortgage was raised to provide Beaumont with money for building. The next 150 years can be described briefly:

1794 Joseph Beaumont sold a small part of his land, retaining the right to build up to his new neighbour's boundary.

1803 Beaumont redeemed his mortgage (perhaps all four houses had been built and were producing a rental income?).

1824 Beaumont's properties, including four cottages at Stonepit End, Wooldale, were devised in trust to provide incomes for his wife, daughters and grandchildren.

1828 Beaumont bought more land in an adjoining village, for building.

1829 Beaumont mortgaged the six acre site, this time to Jonas Hinchcliffe, presumably to pay for the new building, but it is unlikely that this was started, as Beaumont died later that year.

1847 The last surviving trustee of Beaumont's estate, his son-in-law John Eastwood, a dyer, devised the property in trust to his sons Abraham and Edmund Eastwood, and three others.

1886 On the death of Edmund Eastwood the houses passed to Edward Eastwood, son of Abraham.

1887 Following a lawsuit concerning Joseph Beaumont's unredeemed mortgage to Hinchcliffe, Edward Eastwood's copyhold estates were sold to redeem the mortgage.

1888 The four cottages were bought by Joshua Beaumont, a 'scribbling engineer', who may or may not have been related to Joseph Beaumont. One house was then being used as a shop.

1902 On Beaumont's death the cottages passed to his widow and son.

1919 Beaumont's son Tom sold the cottages, now described as 17, 19, 21 and 23, Cinderhills Road, to Joe Heap, who was living at No. 23.

1935 A compensation agreement between Heap and the Lord of the Manor was drawn up in respect of No. 23, and Nos. 17, 19 and 21 were sold at about the same time. By 1950 Heap had become owner of the freehold of No. 23.

The Court Rolls and other documents thus provide a record of ownership over 150 years, from the initial purchase of the site for building. Although there is no exact record of the building date it must almost certainly have been between 1787 and 1803, and probably started in 1794. Nos. 21 and 23 appear to have been built before Nos. 17 and 19, which are simply butted up against their north end. It is interesting to note that the copyholds were granted to the holder, his heirs and assigns 'for ever' rather than for the two or three lives more usual at that time. The rents and entry fines payable to the Lord of the Manor by the copyholders were unchanged in amount from medieval times until the twentieth century, by which time they had become, in real terms, purely nominal sums. The copyholders could apparently sell or mortgage their holdings at will, the resulting security of tenure being in effect little different from a freehold.

The four houses are similar in design, being typical weavers' houses of the period. They appear to have been built in a quarry, hence the old name, Stonepit End. The houses are narrow-fronted, one room wide and two rooms deep, and are three storeys high, the lowest storey being partly sunk into the ground because of the steeply sloping site. The houses were built of the local hard sandstone, with stone slate roofs, and had windows with the heavy square-section mullions typical of the area at the time of building. These windows have survived practically unaltered in Nos. 21 and 23, but in the adjacent Nos. 17 and 19 the mullions have been taken out to allow the insertion of modern 'picture' windows. The entrance, at ground floor level, leads into a kitchen-living room with a small scullery at

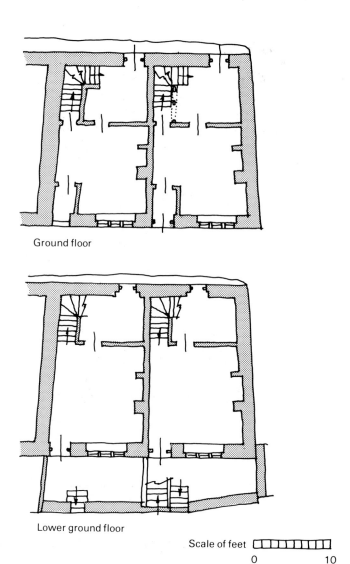

Ground floor

Lower ground floor

Scale of feet

0   10

the rear. From the main room a stone winding stair leads to the upper floors. The first floor also contains two rooms. Both of these may have been bedrooms, but the substantial stone fireplace in the front room suggests that this could have been a parlour. The stone stairs continue to the top floor which comprised the weaving room, extending for the full depth of the house. Rather unusually, this is on two levels, the floor of the front section being raised two steps above that at the rear. The only apparent reason for this would be to provide more headroom in the front

216

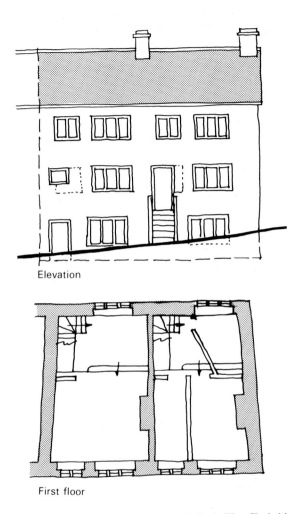

Elevation

First floor

Figs. 60 and 61 **21 and 23 Cinderhills Road, Holmfirth, West Yorkshire.**

room immediately below, again suggesting that this was a living room rather than a bedroom. The headroom in the front part of the weaving room is very low, only about 5 foot 6 inches under the main central roof truss. The weaving room contains a small fireplace, probably intended to regulate the temperature and humidity for weaving rather than for the comfort of the occupants.

In Nos. 21 and 23, but not in the other two houses, a change of plan took place soon after, or even perhaps during their first building. An additional

217

21' Cinderhills Road, Holmfirth, West Yorkshire. The interior of the weaving room on the first floor, now the main living room of the house. Note the low headroom under the main roof beam.

external stair was constructed, leading to the first floor, involving the replacement of a window by a second external door at the higher level. This was probably to allow easier access and transport of wool and finished cloth to and from the weaving room without having to pass through the kitchen area: a feature found in various forms in other weavers' houses. This external stair survives in No. 23, but in No. 21 it has been removed, and the door replaced by a modern window.

It is interesting to note that although these were built as artisans' houses, they were very solidly constructed, and provide quite spacious accommodation, as do many of the weavers' houses of the area. This no doubt is why a considerable number of these houses have survived, and are now becoming popular again. Few of them enjoy the protection of Listing, and in some cases rather unsympathetic alterations are being carried out, such as the removal of the window mullions and insertion of modernistic or fake 'period' doors. It is to be hoped that the growing interest in and appreciation of this early industrial housing will be in time to prevent further unfortunate treatment and secure their preservation.

11
The future of old houses

I suppose it is reasonable to assume that anyone sufficiently interested in old houses to spend time investigating their past history is likely to be concerned about their future. This, however, immediately introduces a new element into our approach. As historians we are simply concerned with finding out facts and recording them. When we start to consider the future of old houses we may have to make decisions, often controversial. What should be preserved and how should this be done? It may perhaps help if we again start by looking at the past, not this time at the history of house design, but at the history of our attitudes to old buildings, and at their legal position today.

During the medieval period there is no evidence of any interest in the preservation of earlier buildings for their own sakes. Houses, like churches, were altered, enlarged or rebuilt in the style of their day to suit the needs of their occupants. On the other hand, wholesale demolition and rebuilding were not universal. Often the best parts of an existing building were retained and adapted, probably on purely economic grounds. With the Renaissance a change in architectural fashion may have given rise to a more drastic rebuilding, but even so, particularly where smaller houses were concerned, a sound building would be retained and altered as necessary.

Only in the nineteenth century do we see the beginning of a desire to preserve old buildings for their own sakes, as historic monuments rather than for economic reasons. This was the age of 'restoration', which, often based on inadequate knowledge coupled with more than adequate funds, was sometimes over-drastic and resulted in loss of authenticity and falsification of the history of the building. Medieval churches suffered much from this process, but houses, particularly the larger ones with wealthy owners, were also affected. Sometimes genuine old work was removed to be replaced by a conjectural restoration of the style of the earliest part of the building.

The future of old houses

39 The Causeway, Steventon, Oxfordshire. A fourteenth century house, later divided into cottages, and suffering progressive deterioration. The roof was partly thatched and partly tiled.

The same house after repair and re-conversion to a single house. In this case it was decided to tile the whole building, since the area had no continuous tradition of thatching. In spite of the dilapidated appearance of the house, much of the main timber-framing had survived.

In the late nineteenth century there was a reaction against this policy, led by such men as John Ruskin, Thomas Carlyle and William Morris, who founded the Society for the Protection of Ancient Buildings in 1876. The alternative put forward by the Society was that restoration should be confined to essential repair, carried out in an honest manner with no attempt to reproduce vanished features, and that an addition to an old building should be recognisable as the work of our own age. The battle between these two extreme points of view was fought long and hard, and is still not entirely resolved today.

At the same time, in the late nineteenth century, the first steps were taken in the protection of historic buildings by the State, with the passing of the first Ancient Monuments Act in 1882. This and subsequent Acts of Parliament gave protection to certain 'Scheduled' Ancient Monuments, but inhabited houses and churches were excluded from their provisions. Only after the Second World War, with the passing of the Town and Country Planning Act of 1947, was any real protection given to the majority of historic buildings, including inhabited houses. Churches were, and still are, largely exempt from this protection.

Under this and subsequent Acts of Parliament Lists of Buildings of Special Architectural or Historic Interest in Britain have been prepared by the Department of Culture, Media and Sport (formerly Dept. of the Environment) for all Local Government Districts. The original Lists were prepared 1950–1960, and revised since, resulting in a considerable increase in listings. The buildings are graded in order of importance, Grade I buildings being those of national importance, and Grade II buildings, the great majority, being those of regional importance. Some buildings coming between these categories are Graded II*; many of these have important interior features not apparent from the exterior.

The Lists, and their accompanying maps, are available for inspection at the County and District Council offices. The owners and occupiers of newly listed buildings are informed of the fact by the District Council. The listing is registered as a Land Charge on the property, and so should be revealed by a Search when a property changes hands.

As there is often misunderstanding of the reasons why buildings are selected for listing, I give below the official criteria adopted by the Department of Culture, Media and Sport, reproduced by permission of H. M. Stationery Office:

All buildings built before 1700 which survive in anything like their original condition are listed. Most buildings of 1700 to 1840 are listed, though selection is necessary. Between 1840 and 1914 buildings must be of definite quality and character to qualify except where they form part of a group, and the selection is designed to include among other buildings the principal works of the principal architects.

A start is now being made on listing a very few selected buildings of 1914 to 1939.

In choosing buildings, particular attention is paid to:

Special value within certain types, either for architectural or planning reasons, or as illustrating social and economic history, (for instance industrial buildings, railway stations, schools, hospitals, theatres, town halls, markets, exchanges, almshouses, prisons, lock-ups, mills).

Technological innovations or virtuosity (for instance, cast iron, prefabrication, or the early use of concrete).

Association with well-known characters or events.

Group value, especially as examples of town planning (for instance squares, terraces or model villages).

Although the revised Lists are far more complete than the original ones, it may still sometimes be found that an unlisted building, of listable quality, is threatened either by demolition or by unsuitable alterations. In these cases the Department may carry out an emergency 'spot-listing'. The same thing may be achieved by the service of a Building Preservation Notice by the District Council, although such a notice has to be confirmed by the Secretary of State for Culture, Media and Sport before it becomes permanently effective.

Once a building has been listed it may not be demolished or altered, externally or internally, in any way that could affect its character, without the consent of the District Council. In all cases involving demolition, and in cases of alterations to Grade I or Grade II* buildings, the Secretary of State has to be notified, and he has the power to call in the application for a Public Inquiry. All applications for demolition or alteration of a listed building have to be advertised, and in cases involving demolition certain national amenity societies have to be notified.

If the owner of a listed building neglects it, perhaps in the hope of obtaining permission for its demolition, the Local Authority may serve a Repairs Notice, requiring certain essential work to be carried out. If the owner fails to comply with this, the Authority may, subject to the approval of the Secretary of State, proceed with Compulsory Purchase. In the case of an unoccupied listed building, the Authority may, as an alternative, carry out certain immediate repairs, and charge the cost to the owner.

In theory, therefore, historic buildings enjoy a considerable amount of protection. In practice, the effectiveness of this depends on the Local Authorities, which may or may not be prepared to take action which could result in considerable public expenditure.

Apart from the provisions affecting individual buildings, whole areas of historic towns and villages may be given some protection by designating them as Conservation Areas. Unlike the compilation of the lists of historic buildings, which is the sole responsibility of the Department of Culture, Media and Sport, the designation of a Conservation Area is carried out by the Planning Authority (the County or District Council), after consultation with the Parish Council and the local community. Apart from other provisions, no building, whether listed or not, may be demolished in a Conservation Area without the consent of the Local Authority, and all such applications have to be advertised.

These provisions may all appear rather negative, and designed to control or even to penalize the owner of a historic building. Recent legislation has, however, also made provision for financial help to be available in certain cases for the repair and maintenance of these buildings. In the case of the nationally important buildings, help may be available from the Government through the English Heritage and the corresponding bodies for Scotland, Wales and Northern Ireland (see page 243). Normally only Grade I and Grade II* buildings are eligible for this help, and the work has to be carried out to an appropriately high standard. There may also be some provision for public access, although this does not always include the interior.

One way in which help from Central Government may be available for less important historic buildings, i.e. Grade II buildings, is through the Townscape Heritage Initiative, which is operated by the Heritage Lottery Fund and a local partnership (generally led by the Local Authority). If an area has both heritage need and economic need and is accepted for the scheme by the Heritage Lottery Fund, a common fund is set up (with the Heritage Lottery Fund contributing 50%) from which grants are offered towards the cost of eligible works undertaken by property owners. The level of grant aid is defined at the start of the scheme, and is fixed in relation to local circumstances. Such schemes have so far been established in only a few areas.

The future of old houses

Bear Steps, Shrewsbury. A group of medieval timber-framed buildings, subsequently plastered over, and fallen into decay. *Right.* **The same group after restoration and conversion to shops, offices and an exhibition hall.**

Local Authorities, County and District Councils may also offer assistance by grant or loan towards the cost of repairs to historic buildings. This is not a mandatory function of the Authorities; it is entirely at their discretion, and Councils vary considerably in the amount of money (if any) made available for this work.

Assistance may also be available from Local Authorities through the various Improvement and Repair Grants offered under the Housing Acts. These grants may be increased above the normal level if the work has to be done in a more expensive way than would otherwise be necessary, because of the historic character of the house. All these grants are at the discretion of the Local Authority, and the owners are means tested to assess the level of grant available. One problem which may arise in connection with Improvement Grants is that the normal conditions attached to them, requiring certain standards to be reached, could result in damage to the historic character of the house; for instance, by enlarging

original windows, or raising ceiling heights. The Local Authorities have the power to relax the standard conditions in these cases but, as with grants, different Councils vary in their approach to these matters. Also, the grants position is constantly changing, and it is always advisable to make contact with the Local Authority to check the current position.

It is also worth noting that a Local Authority has no power to serve a Demolition Order on a listed building by reason of its being unfit for habitation. The Authority may serve a Closing Order, to prevent the house from being occupied until certain remedial works are carried out, but the receipt of such an Order by the owner does not remove the need for him to obtain Listed Building Consent for the work.

From the various legal restrictions just described it might be thought that the owner of a historic house has little choice about alterations and additions to be carried out to it. This is not the case, and much depends on the basic attitude of the owner towards the building. Indeed, it is certain that the owner's views, even more than the amount of money available for the work, decide whether an old house retains its character after modern repairs, alterations or additions have been carried out.

I suppose it is fair to say that there are two extreme attitudes towards an old building. One says, 'This has been here for five hundred years, it is time it was replaced by something better.' The other says, 'This has been here for five hundred years, what right have we mere birds of passage to spoil it?' The latter view was well expressed by William Morris, when he founded the Society for the Protection of Ancient Buildings: 'It has been most truly said that these old buildings do not belong to us alone. That they have belonged to our predecessors and will belong to our descendants unless we play them false. They are in no sense our property, to do as we like with them. We are only trustees for those that come after.' I suppose that most people today would adopt an attitude somewhere between these two extreme views.

As we have seen, until comparatively recent times alterations and additions to old buildings were carried out in the style of the day, with little attempt to copy the original work, although there were always exceptions to the rule. It might therefore be argued that this is the right approach today, and there are probably cases where this is so. Certainly the falsification of the history of a building caused by the heavy-handed Victorian restorations has done irreparable damage in many cases, and this approach is still seen today in the introduction of fake period details.

There are, however, some circumstances today which make it perhaps less desirable in every case to be frankly modern in our treatment of old buildings. In the past, until the advent of mass-production, there was a continuity of tradition in craftsmanship, in spite of change in architectural style and fashion. The builder who inserted Georgian sash windows into a Tudor house had probably worked on such buildings all his life, and may have been a descendant (by family or apprenticeship) of the original builder. The style of the new work might differ from that of the old, but the scale was probably compatible. Today, if new windows are put into an old house they are probably selected from a catalogue of standard designs produced primarily for new buildings, and often quite out of scale with old ones. Simply inserting mock leaded lights, or even so-called Georgian panes, into such windows does not remedy this basic fault.

Also, in the past the need to construct a weathertight pitched roof over a new extension imposed a discipline on the design, so that the new work was related to the original building. Now, the use of flat roofs means that an extension may be of any size and shape, often quite unrelated to the old building. Structurally, too, we have the means to be far more destructive in our alterations. By inserting steel or concrete beams we can remove chimney stacks, or whole walls, or form large openings, all drastically affecting the character of the building. Changed economic conditions, resulting in an increased cost of labour in relation to that of materials, may encourage rebuilding rather than adaptation.

As our old buildings inevitably decrease in number, their value as historic and architectural monuments increases. If a building is to be used today, it may well have to be altered. We cannot expect people today to live in open halls, with unglazed windows, heated by a central hearth, or to share their house with their cattle. However, the fact that we choose to live in an old house when there are far more modern ones available must surely mean that there is something about it that we value and would wish to retain. Something more, that is, than a superficial prettiness.

Much damage is, of course, due simply to ignorance. An old house may well be improved, functionally, by removing comparatively recent work with no resulting historic or architectural damage, but this requires a sound knowledge of the building and its history.

A point of view often expressed today is that, in dealing with old

Prings Cottage, Halling, Kent. A small Wealden house in course of repair after a long period of neglect.

The future of old houses

Prings Cottage after completion of repairs. The roof has been carried over the rebuilt extension, avoiding the flat-roofed treatment all too common today.

buildings, preservation of the facade is all that matters. How often we hear, 'I haven't altered it outside.' I hope that by now the fallacy of this has been made clear: the facade may well be the most recent feature of the building. Historically, the plan form and the roof structure are probably the most significant features of old houses. This must be borne in mind when considering alterations and additions.

Old houses vary greatly in their original design, the extent to which this has survived, and their suitability for use today. Owners also vary in their tastes and in the extent to which they are prepared to adapt their lives to their houses, rather than remodelling their houses to suit their way of life. It is surely true that the more we know and understand about our old houses and their history, the more likely they are to survive and to retain their authentic character. This knowledge and appreciation, even more than increasingly stringent legislation, is probably the best hope for their future.

Appendix I

The measured survey

As pointed out in Chapter 8, one of the best ways of working out the historical development of a house is by carrying out a careful measured survey. This is even more essential if we are planning alterations.

The equipment needed is as follows:

1 A sketch pad, or plain or squared paper, and a firm clip board.

2 A 100 foot (or metric equivalent) linen or steel tape. Steel tapes are more accurate as linen tapes tend to stretch with age, but a steel tape is more easily damaged and more difficult to handle. Normally a linen tape is satisfactory provided that the same tape is used for the whole building.

3 A 5 foot expanding wooden rod or a 6 foot or 10 foot retractable tape of the type that stays rigid when opened.

For drawing up the survey it is best to work on a drawing board with a T-square and set-square. Small portable drawing boards are now available, quite suitable for this purpose. Adjustable-angle set-squares are particularly useful as old buildings are rarely true and square. A set of drawing instruments will provide compasses, with an extension piece for large dimensions, and spring-bows for very small dimensions and for showing door swings if required. A 6 inch scale will also be needed, graded in imperial or metric scales. For the survey and the final drawing either imperial or metric measurements can be used.

A survey of a small simple building can be carried out single-handed, but it is far more satisfactory if two, or better still three, people can take part. This enables the tape to be kept taut and more accurate measurements to be taken, with one person holding the tape, the second measuring, and the third noting down the dimensions.

The scale to be used for the final drawings will depend upon the size of the building and the amount of detail required. Normally a scale of 1:100 or 8 feet to 1 inch is used for larger buildings, and 1:50 or 4 feet to 1 inch for smaller buildings, or where it is desired to show details of timber-framing or other construction.

The first step is to sketch out the plans of each floor of the house. Until experience is gained, it may be helpful to use squared paper and to pace out the main dimensions of each room before sketching it out. With practice, however, it becomes fairly easy to sketch out a room approximately to scale.

It is important to show all wall thicknesses. Amateur survey plans often omit these, indicating walls by a single line only. Windows and doorways should be shown, and features such as built-up openings and straight joints should be marked on the plan, as should beams, fireplaces, changes in the direction of walls, and changes of floor level and material. The spacing of the roof trusses should be shown on the top-floor plan.

After sketching out the floor plans, one or more cross sections should be sketched, showing the roof construction where this is visible, and any features such as crucks or aisle posts. The external elevations should also be sketched.

Having completed this work, the actual measuring can be started. In each room, dimensions should be taken along each wall, working clockwise, i.e. from left to right. Dimensions should always be taken 'running', that is, measured from the left hand end of the wall. This avoids the risk of cumulative errors which could occur if separate short measurements were taken. Window measurements are usually taken at the jambs (the edges of the opening), but if the reveals are splayed, both outer and inner measurements should be taken. At door openings the measurements are usually taken to the door opening, rather than to the frame. The important thing is to take measurements to the same point on both sides of the wall.

After measuring the walls of the room, diagonal measurements should be taken. This is particularly important in old buildings, which are often out of square. The aim should be to build up the plan as a series of triangles. In theory, one diagonal across the room should be sufficient, but it is better to take them both as a check on any error in measuring. Diagonals should also be taken to fix any point where a wall changes direction, and to any free-standing columns or posts.

As well as measuring each separate room in this way, and measuring wall thicknesses at door and window openings, it is helpful if long measurements can be taken for the whole length and breadth of the building — along a corridor, or through inter-communicating rooms.

To draw up the sections and elevations of the house it is necessary to measure the ceiling heights in each room, window cill and head heights,

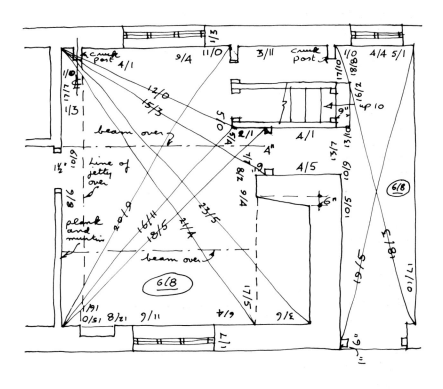

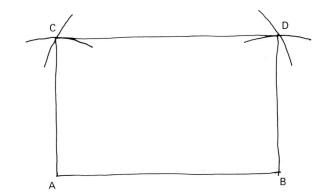

Fig. 62 **Drawing up the plan of a room; the measured survey. Sketch survey of part of ground floor of 18 and 19 West Orchard, Dorset.**

and door head heights. Floor thicknesses should be measured at staircase wells, and changes of floor level should be noted. If the rooms on the upper floor are partly in the roof space, or if the roof space is accessible, it is usually easy to obtain the angle of pitch of the roof by measuring the height to the ridge. If the roof construction is original, or early, the sizes and positions of the timbers should be shown and measured. If the roof space is not accessible, it may be possible to measure the height of the ridge externally, on the end gable wall.

In the case of a brick building, heights can be obtained by counting the brick courses. In modern work, brickwork rises four courses to one foot, but in old buildings this varies considerably and it is therefore necessary to measure a sample area and to use this to calculate other heights.

Photographs are of great help in a survey. External views should be as near to true elevations as possible. Angled views are of less use

Apart from the main plans, sections and elevations, detailed drawings should be made of features such as early doors and windows, and moulded beams.

When the survey is complete, the next task is drawing it up. It is best to do this on tracing paper, so that when the ground-floor plan has been drawn, the upper floors can be traced over it as a check on the measurements. (It must be remembered, however, that old walls are not always strictly plumb.) The method of drawing up is shown in fig. 62. First, draw the line A–B to the required scale. Then, using compasses, describe an arc the length of the side wall A–C, and another the length of the diagonal B–C. This fixes point C. Point D is fixed similarly, and the length C–D checked from the survey measurements. By taking one more dimension than is strictly necessary you are able to check if there has been an error in one of them.

The whole ground-floor plan is drawn up in this way, followed by the upper floors, sections and elevations. If tracing paper has been used, photoprints may be obtained from the finished tracing.

From the finished drawing, and our general study of the house, it is often possible to pick out the original form of the building, and the various subsequent alterations and additions, especially if such features as changes in wall thickness and direction, straight joints, and changes in the roof line have been marked. It may even be possible to produce a series of sketch plans showing the building at different stages of its development, although we must beware of conjectural restorations and wishful thinking! The basic survey drawing can also be used as a base, to note any features which may be uncovered in the course of alterations to the house.

If the house is of any historic interest, the local museum, local historical society, and the Record Office will probably be grateful for copies of the finished drawings, and a set should also be kept with the deeds of the house for the benefit of future owners.

A cottage built on a small enclosure on the edge of heathland at Winfrith, Dorset, c 1750. In the Manorial Court Roll for December 1773, it is recorded that John Trent took a Copyhold tenancy of this cottage, described as 'some time since built and taken in from the Waste at Black Nool within the said Manor.' The tenancy was granted on the lives of John, then aged 33, and his sons Jonathan, aged 13 and John, aged 10, at a yearly rent of two shillings.

Appendix II

Glossary

Aisled Hall A hall, the main living area of a house, divided into three (or occasionally two) aisles by arcades (lines of posts and arches supporting the roof). The arcades in houses are generally of timber, but are occasionally of stone, as in a church.

Architrave In Classical architecture, the lowest member of the entablature, immediately above the columns. In domestic building, the moulding covering the joint between a door or window frame and the adjoining wall face.

Ashlar *a* Stone cut into smooth rectangular blocks and laid with fine joints in regular courses.
b In an attic room, timber studding, normally plastered, cutting off the angle between the roof line and the floor.

Baluster A vertical stone or timber member, often turned, supporting a handrail or capping, as on a staircase or balustrade.

Bargeboard *(or verge board)* A timber board, often moulded or carved, fixed to the verge of a roof. Originated in timber-framed construction, where it covered the exposed ends of the purlins and wall plates; it was later used also on brick and stone buildings, particularly in the nineteenth century.

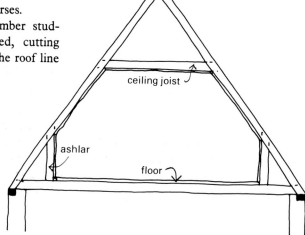

Fig. 63 **Ashlaring in an attic room**

234

Bay The space between two roof trusses, or between the truss and end wall of a building or room. Also used to describe the vertical divisions of a facade, by pilasters or windows.

Bond The pattern of laying bricks in walling. *English Bond* consists of alternate courses of headers (bricks laid at right angles to the wall line) and stretchers (bricks laid parallel to the wall line). *Flemish Bond* consists of alternate headers and stretchers in each course. See page 146.

Box-frame construction Timber-framed construction in which the walls support the roof and the upper floors, the whole structure being framed together. See page 46.

Braces Timber members, often curved, linking horizontal and vertical members in a roof or wall, to strengthen the joint between them and prevent distortion of the framing.

Buttery A service room for the storage of drink.

Byre A building to house animals, either a separate building or the lower end of a long-house.

Chamfer A splay, cutting off the outer angles of a beam, a door or window jamb, or a window mullion. See page 175.

Closed string stair A stair in which the treads and risers are framed into the string and their ends concealed by it. See page 177.

Cob A primitive form of concrete made of chalk, mud and chopped straw.

Collar beam A beam connecting a pair of principal or common rafters at some distance above their feet.

Collar purlin A longitudinal timber joining a series of collars at their centres in a trussed rafter roof.

Common rafters Pairs of rafters forming a pitched roof, either supported on purlins and trusses, or framed in a trussed rafter roof.

Fig. 66 **Console (e.g. to a door opening)**

Console A carved or moulded bracket supporting a door hood or canopy.

Cornice In Classical architecture, the top member of the entablature. In domestic building, a moulding at the junction of the wall and the ceiling in a room, or a moulding on an external wall at the eaves line.

235

Glossary

Crown post A vertical post rising from a tie-beam in a roof to support a collar purlin. See page 27.

Crucks Large curved timbers supporting a roof from the ground, without the need for load-bearing walls. See page 134.

Cut string stair A stair in which the string is cut away to allow the ends of the treads and risers to be seen. The nosing of the tread is usually returned round its ends as a capping to the string at tread level. See page 177.

Dado Panelling on the lower part of an internal wall, usually extending to about 3 feet above floor level.

Dais A raised platform, particularly at the upper end of a hall.

Dog-leg stair A stair formed in two flights, the upper flight returned alongside the lower flight, with a half-space landing at the junction of the flights. See page 176.

Double-hung sash window A timber window consisting of two vertical sliding sashes, operated by counter-weights concealed in a boxed frame.

Double-pile plan A plan of a house two rooms deep under a single span roof. See page 85.

End hall house A house with a hall and one two-storeyed block only, containing service rooms on

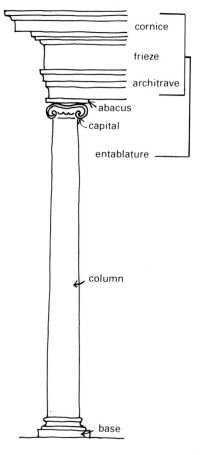

Fig. 64 **Classical architectural details (based on the Ionic Order). The classical 'Orders', introduced after the Renaissance, were freely adapted by the builders of smaller and medium sized houses.**

the ground floor and a solar on the first-floor.

Entablature The structure supported by a column or collonade, divided in Classical architecture and most Classical reconstructions into three horizontal bands, architrave, frieze and cornice.

236

Facade The main external elevation of a building.

First-floor hall house A house where the main living area, the hall, is on the first floor, and is often approached by an external stair. See page 29.

Four-centred arch An arch struck from four centres, in use from the later fifteenth to the mid seventeenth centuries, sometimes called a Tudor arch. See page 151.

Frieze In Classical architecture, the centre member of the entablature. In domestic building a band, sometimes ornamented, at the top of a wall below the ceiling or cornice.

Glazing bars Bars dividing window sashes into smaller panes.

Hall In early houses, the main living area. In later periods the hall declined in importance and eventually became the entrance vestibule.

Husbandman The smaller farmer of late medieval and Tudor times, less well off and holding less land than the yeoman.

Hipped roof A roof of which the slopes rise from the eaves on all sides of the building, i.e. without gables; the hip being the junction between two adjoining slopes.

Hood mould (*or weather mould*) A projecting moulding over the head of a door or window opening, designed to protect the opening from rainwater running down the wall face.

Jamb The side of a door or window opening.

Jetty An overhanging wall in timber-framed construction. Usually an external feature, it is occasionally found internally in open hall houses. See page 118.

Jointed-cruck truss A roof truss in which the crucks are formed in two sections, jointed at or near the eaves line. See page 163.

Joists The smaller timber beams carrying a floor or ceiling. In small rooms they may span between the walls, but in larger rooms they are carried on main beams.

King-post A vertical timber member rising from a tie-beam in a roof to support the ridge piece. See page 46.

Laithe house A later development of the long-house where the byre, or the barn, still attached to the house, is not connected with it internally.

Lintel A beam spanning an opening, of a doorway, a window or a fireplace.

Listed building A building included in the Statutory Lists of Buildings of Special Architectural or Historic Interest. See page 221.

Long-house An early type of house, divided into a living area and a byre for animals, usually with opposed doors, and sometimes a through passage between the two sections. See page 45.

Louvre *a* A horizontal slat inserted at an angle in an unglazed window to prevent the entry of driving rain.
b A turret in the roof of an open hall, sited above the hearth, to allow smoke to escape.

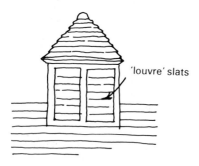

'louvre' slats

Mansard roof A roof having two pitches, that of the lower part of the roof being steeper than that of the upper slope. See page 82.

Matchboarding Timber boarding, grooved and tongued at the edges to fit together as a covering for walls and, less often, for ceilings.

Mathematical tiling Special tiles used for vertical cladding, made to resemble brickwork and pointed as for brickwork after fixing.

Mullion A vertical stone or timber member dividing a window into sections, known as lights.

Muntin A vertical intermediate framing member in a door, or in panelling.

Newel post *a* The central post of a spiral or newel stair.
b The main vertical framing member in a straight-flight, dog-leg, or open-well stair. Newel posts are often finished with ornamental caps and pendants.

Newel stair A spiral stair where the treads and risers (or solid steps, in early examples) are framed into a central newel post.

Ogee arch An arch formed with a reversed curve, giving an S-shaped profile. See page 151.

Open field system The medieval system of arable farming in Britain. Surrounding the village were normally three large open fields, divided

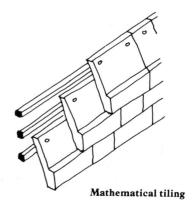

Mathematical tiling

into narrow strips, allocated to the various farmers in the village. The holdings of each farmer were distributed over the fields, which were farmed in common. Two of the fields grew different crops each year, while the third lay fallow to maintain a system of crop rotation. As a common system of farming it was brought to an end by the Enclosures which were effected from the sixteenth to the eighteenth centuries.

Oriel A projecting bay window at ground or an upper floor level. In the late medieval manor house, the oriel at the upper end of the hall eventually developed into a small projecting room or alcove.

Pantile A single lap roofing tile with an S-shaped profile.

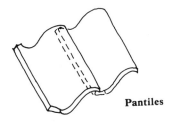

Pantiles

Pantry A service room for the storage of food (originally bread).

Parapet A wall extending above a roof, at the eaves or at a gable.

Parlour A 'withdrawing' room leading off the hall. In early houses it was generally used for sleeping, and later it became a private living room.

Pediment A shallow triangular, or occasionally arched, head to a door or window opening, derived from the shallow pitched gable end of the classical temple. See page 86.

Pentice, an open-fronted shelter.

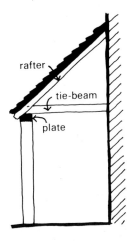

Pentice A lean-to open shelter, or a porch of similar design.

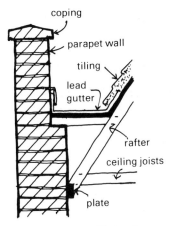

Parapet

239

Glossary

Pilaster A half-column fixed against a wall, often framing a door opening. See page 78.

Pitch *(roof)* The angle of the roof slope.

Plank and muntin An early form of timber partition consisting of vertical members (muntins) linked by thinner planks slotted into the grooved edges of the muntins. See page 170.

Plinth A projecting moulding at the base of an external wall, column or pier.

Principal rafters The main rafters in a roof truss, supporting the purlins and the ridge piece. See page 46.

Purlin A main horizontal member in a roof, supporting the common rafters and carried on the principal rafters of the trusses. See page 46.

Queen post roof A roof where the trusses have two vertical members supporting the principal rafters, rising from the tie-beam, and generally tied at their heads by a collar beam.

Quoin *a* The corner of a building. *b* The stones forming the corner of a building, often larger than those in the rest of the wall and sometimes ornamented or raised.

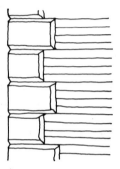

Quoins – raised stone quoins used in a brick building.

Rail A horizontal framing member in a door, or in panelling.

Reveal The side of an opening in a wall for a window or door.

Ridge The upper intersection of the main slopes of a roof.

Ridge piece or beam A beam forming the ridge of the roof, supporting the tops of the common rafters, and itself supported on the main trusses.

Rubble Roughly cut stone in a wall. It may be laid in courses or

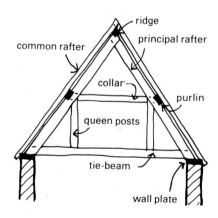

Queen-post roof

240

completely random laid. The joints are thicker than those in ashlar work and the whole effect coarser and less regular.

Scheduled Ancient Monument A building, monument or earthwork, which may not be demolished or altered without the consent of the Department of the Environment. Inhabited houses do not qualify for this kind of scheduling.

Screens passage The passage at the lower end of a hall, separated from the hall by a screen rather than a solid wall. See pages 38 and 39.

Shingles Thin slabs of timber, usually oak, used for roofing, similarly to slates or tiles. In modern work cedar is often used.

Shouldered arch A mock arch formed by shaped timber posts or stone jambs supporting a lintel. See page 151.

Single-pile plan The plan of a house one room deep. See page 56.

Skirting A moulding at the base of an internal wall.

Smoke bay The first improvement to the open hearth in an open hall. The upper part of the central truss in a two-bay hall or, in a larger hall, the truss nearest one end wall, was filled in to channel the smoke towards the louvre.

Solar A private withdrawing room, used for sleeping or as a living room, at first-floor level. (Literally, the 'room above the floor'.)

Spere truss The truss at the lower end of a hall, retaining aisle posts and framing the screen.

Stile The outer vertical framing member in a door.

String The outer member of a staircase, into which the treads and risers are framed. See page 177.

String course A continuous moulding on an external wall, often at an upper floor level, dividing the facade into storey heights.

Strut An alternative name for a brace (q.v.), but generally used of straight timbers.

Studs, studding Vertical timber members in a wall or partition.

Tie-beam A beam joining the feet of a pair of principal rafters in a roof truss. See page 46.

Truss A framed structure supporting a roof, consisting of a pair of principal rafters, secured by a tie-beam or a collar beam, supporting purlins which in turn support the common rafters.

Trussed rafter roof A roof without main trusses, but generally with tie-beams at intervals. Each pair of rafters is joined by a collar. Sometimes there are struts between the collar and the rafters.

241

Glossary

Turnpike road A road constructed and maintained by a Turnpike Trust, which had the right to collect tolls from users of the road to pay for this work. Most such trusts were founded in the eighteenth century, and they gradually died out after the late nineteenth century, as the Local Authorities became responsible for the roads.

Two-centred arch A Gothic (pointed) arch struck from two centres. See page 151.

Vault *a* An underground chamber, also one used for burials.
b An arched ceiling constructed of stone or, less often, of brick found for instance in cellars and the undercrofts of some first-floor hall houses.

Verges see *Bargeboard*

Wattle and daub The earliest form of infilling to timber-framed partitions and walls. Vertical timber rods were inserted into holes and grooves in the horizontal framing members. Willow or hazel withies were woven round these, basket fashion, and the whole finished with a 'daub' of clay, chalk and mud, with a final coat of lime plaster.

Wealden house A late medieval and Tudor form of open hall house of small or medium size, based on the plan of the larger house. The name is derived from the Weald of Kent and Sussex, where some of the best examples are found. See page 49.

Weather mould See *Hood mould*

Wind bracing Curved braces in the plane of the sloping faces of a roof, linking the trusses and the purlins. Originally intended to prevent the roof distorting, they became an ornamental feature of the design.

Wind bracing in a roof

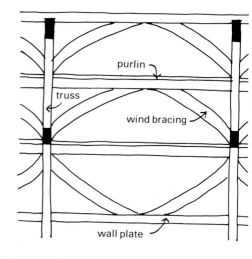

Yeomen The wealthier farmer of later medieval and Tudor times. below the rank of 'gentleman'. He might be a freeholder, or a wealthy tenant farmer, holding his land with security of tenure.

242

Appendix III

Organisation concerned with old houses

Central government organisations in Britain

Department of Culture Media and Sport, 2–4 Cockspur Street, London SW1Y 5DH. 0171-211 6000. The Department issues the Statutory Lists of Buildings of Special Architectural and Historic Interest, which are prepared on the advice of English Heritage. Requests for permission to alter or demolish listed buildings are determined by local planning authorities, and any resulting appeals by the Department of Environment, Transport and the Regions.

English Heritage, 23 Savile Row, London W1X 2HAE. 0171-973 3000 English Heritage is the Government's statutory adviser on all aspects of the historic environment. In 1999 it was amalgamated with the Royal Commission on the Historical Monuments of England, which has to be given the opportunity to inspect and record any listed building in advance of its demolition.

Historic Scotland, Longmore House, Salisbury Place, Edinburgh EH9 1SH. 0131-668 8600
Cadw: Welsh Historic Monuments, Crown Building, Cathays Park, Cardiff CF1 3NQ. 01222 500200
Department of the Environment for Northern Ireland, Environment and Heritage Service, Commonwealth House, 35 Castle Street, Belfast BT1 1GU. 01232 251477
These bodies provide advice on the giving of financial assistance for the repair of historic buildings, including houses. Normally only Grade I and Grade II* buildings are eligible for assistance, but Grade II buildings may receive help under Town Schemes, or in Conservation Areas.

Heritage Lottery Fund, 7 Holbein Place, London SW1W 8NR
0171-591 6000. The HLF operates through the National Heritage

Organisations concerned with old houses

Memorial Fund. It provides grants from the National Lottery which can include assistance with the restoration of historic buildings.

National Monuments Records for England, Scotland and Wales
The following hold large publically accessible databases and archives of the historic buildings (and archaeological sites) of their respective countries.
England: National Monuments Record Centre, Kemble Drive, Swindon SN2 2GZ. 01793 414600
Scotland: John Sinclair House, 16 Bernard Terrace, Edinburgh, EH8 9NX. 0131-662 1456
Wales: Crown Buildings, Plas Crug, Aberystwyth, Cardigan, SY23 1NJ. 01970 621233

Voluntary organisations

Ancient Monuments Society St Ann's Vestry Hall, 2 Church Entry, London EC4V 5HB. 0171-236 3934. An organisation with similar aims and objectives to those of the Society for the Protection of Ancient Buildings. Publishes annual transactions concerned with architectural history.

Architectural Heritage Fund 27 John Adams Street, London WC2N 6HX. 0171-925 0199. A charity administered by the Civic Trust. Provides short-term loan capital to help Buildings Preservation Trusts acquire, restore and re-sell threatened historic buildings.

Civic Trust 17 Carlton House Terrace, London SW1Y 5AW. 0171-930 0914. Is concerned with all aspects of civic design. Advises and co-ordinates the work of affiliated local civic and amenity societies. Prepares and issues booklets, exhibitions and films. Has advised the Department of the Environment Regions and Transport on the drafting of conservation legislation. Gives awards for good design, including work on historic buildings.

Council for British Archaeology Bowes Morrell House, 111 Walmgate, York YO1 2UA. 01904-671417. Acts as a link between local archaeological societies and the relevant government organisations, and provides information on all aspects of British Archaeology.

Council for the Protection of Rural England Warwick House, 25 Buckingham Palace Road, London SW1W 0PP. 0171-976 6433, and

Campaign for the Protection of Rural Wales, Ty Gwyn, 31 High Street,

Welshpool, Powys, SG21 7GD, Wales 01938-552525/556212 (Also have branches in all parts of the country.)
Are concerned with all aspects of the countryside, including rural housing.

Georgian Group 6 Fitzroy Square, London W1P 6DX. 0171-387 1720
Originally a sub-committee of the Society for the Protection of Ancient Buildings. Now a separate body doing similar work in respect of Georgian buildings.

Historic Houses Association 2 Chester Street, London SW1X 7BB.
0171-259 5688. An association of owners of historic houses, with the aim of preserving such houses, gardens and parks.

Landmark Trust Shottesbrook, Maidenhead, Berkshire SL6 3SW.
01628 825920. Aims to save smaller historic buildings by acquiring and repairing them. Most of the Trust's properties are let as holiday accommodation.

The National Trust 36 Queen Anne's Gate, London SW1H 9AS.
0171-222 9251
The National Trust for Scotland 5 Charlotte Square, Edinburgh EH2 4DU.
0131-226 5922
Own a large number of properties, mostly larger houses but including a number of smaller houses, particularly those with historic connections.

Society for the Protection of Ancient Buildings 37 Spital Square, London E1 6DY. Tel: 0171-377 1644. Provides technical advice on repairs and alterations to historic buildings. Organises conferences and courses on this subject, and awards an annual scholarship. May advise on sources of financial help. Issues lists of threatened buildings for sale or lease (to members only).

UK Association of Buildings Preservation Trusts Clareville House, 26–27 Oxenden Street, London SW1Y 4EL. 0171-930 1629. Established in 1989 by the Architectural Heritage Fund with which it works in tandem. A government-aided charity, it promotes the work of Building Preservation Trusts to find long-term, sustainable solutions to problem buildings. Also provides practical help and advice, and publishes guidance notes and newsletters.

Vernacular Architecture Group 16 Falna Crescent, Coton Green, Tamworth, Staffordshire B79 8JS. Promotes the study of smaller houses and cottages, as well as farm and early industrial buildings.

Organisations concerned with old houses

Victorian Society 1 Priory Gardens, Bedford Park, London W4 1TT. 0181-994 1019. Also originally a sub-committee of the Society for the Protection of Ancient Buildings. Now a separate body doing similar work in respect of nineteenth and early twentieth century buildings.

In addition to the national organisations, local authority conservation officers, local historical, civic and amenity societies may provide help and advice for owners of old houses. Their addresses are usually available at the local public library. Local museums may also provide information.

The Lists of Buildings of Special Architctural or Historic Interest, compiled by the Department for Culture, Media and Sport, may be inspected at the offices of the Local Planning Authorities (County and District Councils) or, for England, through the central computerised lists maintained by The National Monuments Record.

Bibliography

Chapter 1 *The story of your house*

Harvey, John H. *Sources for the History of Houses*. London, 1974
Hoskins, W.G. *Fieldwork in Local History*. London, 1967
Melling, Elizabeth Ed: *Some Kentish Houses*. Maidstone, 1965
Rogers, Alan *Approaches to Local History*. London, 1978

Chapter 2 *Medieval Foundations*

Fox, Sir Cyril and Raglan, Lord *Monmouthshire Houses*. Vol. I. National Museum of Wales, 1951–4
Platt, Colin *The English Medieval Town*. London, 1976
Wood, Margaret *The English Medieval House*. London, 1965

Chapter 3 *Tudor Revolution*

Barley, M.W. *The English Farmhouse and Cottage*. London, 1976
Fox, Sir Cyril and Raglan, Lord *Monmouthshire Houses*. Vol II. National Museum of Wales, 1951–4
Mercer, Eric *English Vernacular Houses*. HMSO, 1975

Chapter 4 *The Last Three Hundred Years*

Cruickshank, D. and Wyld, P. *London, the Art of Georgian Building*. London, 1977
Lowe, J.B. *Welsh Industrial Workers' Housing. 1775-1875*. Cardiff, 1977
Summerson, John *Georgian London*. London 1979

Chapter 5 *Changes in Status and Function*

Godfrey, W.E. *The English Almshouse*. London, 1955

Bibliography

Chapter 6 *Travellers' Houses*

Johnson, W. Branch 'Some sources of Inn History', in *The Local Historian*
Richardson, A.E. *The Old Inns of England*. London, 1938
Richardson, A. E. and Eberlein, H. D. *The English Inn Past and Present*. London, 1925

Chapters 7 and 8 *Historical Survey of a House*

Ayres, Jane *Shell Book of the Home in Britain*. London, 1981
Brunskill, R.W. *Illustrated Handbook of Vernacular Architecture*. London, 1978
Clifton-Taylor, Alec *The Pattern of English Building*. London, 1977

Chapter 11 *The Future of Old Houses*

Briggs, Martin S. *Goths and Vandals*. London, 1952
Christian, R. *Vanishing Britain*. Newton Abbot, 1977
Cunnington, P.M. *Care for Old Houses*. Sherborne, 1984
Godfrey, W.H. *Our Building Inheritance*. London, 1954
Insall, D.W. *The Care of Old Buildings*. London, 1958

General

Baker, Alan H. and Hartley J.B. Eds: *Man made The Land*. Newton Abbot, 1973
Barley, M.W. *The House and Home*. London, 1963
Batsford and Fry *The English Cottage*. London, 1938
Brunskill, R.W. *Houses*. London, 1982
Hoskins, W.G. *English Landscapes*. London, 1973
Lloyd, Nathaniel *A History of the English House*. London, 1975
Pevsner, N. *The Buildings of England* (County Series). Harmondsworth, 1951 seqq.
Trevelyan, G.M. *English Social History*. London, 1945, 1978
Volumes of the Survey of the Royal Commission on Historical Monuments of England. The following counties and smaller areas have been surveyed to date: Buckinghamshire, City of Cambridge, West and North-east Cambridgeshire, Dorset, Essex, Gloucestershire (Iron Age and Romano-British Cotswolds), Herefordshire, Hertfordshire, Huntingdonshire, Stamford in Lincolnshire, London, Middlesex, Northamptonshire (North-east, Central, North-west and South-west archaeological sites, archaeological sites and churches in Northampton,

North Architectural monuments), City of Oxford, Peterborough New Town, Westmorland, City of Salisbury (Wiltshire), Yorkshire (Roman York, other monuments in South-west, East and Central Yorkshire). Other publications on old houses by the Royal Commission include Shielings and Bastles; York, Historic Buildings in the Central Area; Early Industrial Housing, the Trinity Area of Frome; Beverley; Rural Houses of West Yorkshire, 1400-1830; Workers' Houses in West Yorkshire, 1750-1920; Rural Houses of the Lancashire Pennines; Non-conformist Chapels & Meeting Houses in Central England, South-West England and the North of England; Houses of the North Yorks Moors; Whitehaven, a New Town of the Late 17th Century; English Houses 1200–1800: the Hertfordshire Evidence; Salisbury: the Houses of the Close; The Medieval Houses of Kent: an Historic Analysis; The Country Houses of Northamptonshire; English Farmsteads 1750–1914.

The photographic archives of the National Monuments Record include Farms in England, prehistoric to present, and Yesterday's Gardens. Similar Surveys in Scotland and Wales cover Berwickshire, Caithness, Dumfriesshire, East Lothian, City of Edinburgh, Fife, Kinross and Clackmannan, Galloway (Kirkcudbrightshire, Galloway), Wigtownshire, Mid and West Lothian, Orkney and Shetland, Outer Hebrides, Peebleshire, Roxburghshire, Selkirk, Stirlingshire, Sutherland, Anglesey, Caernarvonshire, Carmarthenshire, Denbighshire, Flintshire, Merioneth, Montgomeryshire, Pembrokeshire, Radnorshire.

It will be appreciated that most of these Surveys were prepared before the reorganisation of Local Government in 1974, and are published under the old county names and boundaries. In the earlier Surveys no buildings or monuments later in date than 1715 are included. In more recent Surveys the date limit is 1850.

Survey of London. Formerly published by the Greater London Council, and now being continued by the Royal Commission on Historical Monuments. Forty-four volumes had been published by 1999. Most of these are based on the ancient London parishes.

Index

Index

Acknowledgements

I should like to thank all those who have helped me in this work, and in particular the following house owners who have given permission for their houses to be described and illustrated.

The Weymouth Civic Society: 2 and 3, Trinity St, Weymouth, Dorset*

The Landmark Trust, and the Architectural and Planning Partnership: Purton Green Farm, Stansfield, Suffolk*

The North Bedfordshire Borough Council: Bunyan's Mead, Elstow, Bedfordshire*

The Ruddington Framework Knitters' Shops Preservation Trust: Framework Knitters' Houses, Chapel St, Ruddington, Notts*

Mrs M. Henley: Red Lion Inn, Southampton, Hants

Sir Claude J. Hayes: Prinkham, Chiddingstone, Kent

The National Trust, and the Royal Pavilion, Art Gallery and Museums, Brighton; Blaise Hamlet, Bristol

Mr R. Myott: Churche's Mansion, Nantwich, Cheshire*

Mr Beevor: Saint John's, Hinton Martel, Dorset

Mr D.H.C. Crane: The Potash, Cretingham Suffolk

Mrs E. Cocks: 18 and 19, West Orchard, Dorset

Dr J. Ogilvie: Thorn House, Hartsop, Cumbria

Mr P. Lorimer: 21, Cinderhills Rd, Holmfirth, West Yorks

Mrs Edwards: 23, Cinderhills Rd, Holmfirth, West Yorks

Mr and Mrs H. C. Dance: The Old Vicarage, Methwold, Norfolk

The Weald and Downland Museum, Singleton, Sussex: Wealden Hall House*

The National Trust: Lower Brockhampton, Hereford and Worcestershire*; Treasurer's House, Martock, Somerset*

Kingston Lacy and Corfe Castle Estates: Lodge Farm, Pamphill